His mom?

BROKEN BANANAH

BY ROSS ASDOURIAN

female doctor?

BROKEN BANANAH

First edition. April 11, 2018.

ISBN-13:978-1986101882

Written By Ross Asdourian.

DEDICATION

———

Thank you to all the family, friends, and medical staff that quite literally kept me together through this.

Special thank you to my army of friend editors, led by Ellyn and Carolina, for bearing with unrelenting tense changes.
Thank you to Byron for bringing my banana to life.
...on the cover, relax.

———

**The following is a true story.
Not "based on" either.
This all really happened.**

CONTENTS

BEFORE PLAY

It can always be worse. Remember that. It can always be worse.
It's still attached. It can always be worse.
It *could* always be worse? It can always be worse.

That was the phrase that repeated in my head, staring down at what can only be described as a pulsing eggplant between my legs. Love is a battlefield, and the blanket laying over my lap hid the world from the true horror of my broken penis.

The clock ticked. Nikki had run out of places to stare at in the emergency room.

"I can't believe this is happening," she said with that sort of wide-eyed, one-huff mini laugh.

"I'll marry you, I really will. I swear." A knock at the door interrupted this matter-of-fact proposal. Pretty much every time a doctor knocks on the door, I immediately act like I wasn't doing whatever I was doing. As though the doctor would give me better care if I wasn't on my phone or staring at the weird anatomy posters that are somehow in every doctor's office. I'll admit it. I usually do fantasize about stashing a bunch of medical supplies from the blue drawers. This would, of course, save money when I'd need a handful of alcohol wipes or sterile gloves.

"Hi Ross, how are you feeling?" he asked.

"Never been better!" I answered with an ironic amount of zest. Dr. Casey held the test results with the fate of my children and my children's children close to his chest. He took a peek under the hood and marvelled over the size of my swelling johnson. All things aside, this was something I could get used to.

The doctor took a quick glance at Nikki and then back at me. I gave him the universal nod of approval and smiled at Nikki right after. She was still there and, in an odd way, her presence meant something. I wanted her there despite the fact that we didn't really know each other. Our last encounter dated back seven years to a party in Gainesville, Florida. We were just as much intimate strangers then as we were now. She scooted her chair closer as Dr. Casey shuffled a thin pile of papers and, with a discernible amount of trained empathy, began his speech.

"In situations like this," he explained, "it's difficult to know exactly what's happening without having a look inside." My smile grew larger to mask the acceptance of bad news I felt coming. Then I made a request. A request that anyone in a traumatic hospital situation can't help but ask.

"What's the best case and worst case scenario?"

A rhetorical question really. Best case is that everything's back to normal. Worst case is that nothing ever works again. Right? Except that when Dr. Casey delivered the bad news, he gave it that little extra detail that psychologists may, years later, deem wildly unnecessary.

"You'll lose functionality and sensitivity. Given that you aren't able to urinate on your own, there is a possibility that the damage to your urethra will require a tube which we would surgically implant to relieve your bladder. This is, of course, worst case, but do want you to be aware."

So there I was, foreseeably castrated. I looked at Nikki, silently hysterical, as she imagined a future with a dickless husband while I lay there thinking about the worst part. How am I going to tell Parker -- the girl who I was thinking about, but not the girl who I'd just had sex with.

1

SEX GHOSTS

I have a love/hate relationship with Facebook. The love comes from all the friends and family it allows me to keep in touch with, which can be tough even with those who we're closest with. The hate comes from all the ex-girlfriends that won't go away. The part that I'm indifferent to is how Facebook keeps past, current, and prospective sexual partners one message away. This is important for people who, like me, live in the Big Apple, a city where most people are either visiting soon or want to.

New York City alienates even the most popular, and like many of us, I'm alone more than I care to be. That sounds depressing as shit, but for now let's blame that for what happened next. I do what everyone does when there's nothing to do, open and close the same website window within minutes hoping for a new notification. I do it on my phone too by checking for messages even though there hasn't even been a notification. Parker calls those phantom vibrations, but I'm clearly not thinking about her right now. I'm fixated on the red bubble over the Facebook Messenger tab.

Nikki
> 10:52am: yo!
> 10:53am: i'm in new york. i hear you're living here now :)
> maybe we should catch up.

All lower case is an odd anti-establishment thing some people do. I don't get it, but sometimes i do it too. The key part of her message was right in the middle. She stuck that smiley face in, and I knew it was on. Some people would argue it's just a smiley face and nothing more than cordial. I would agree, but the last time we talked was in college seven years ago while hooking up, which I define as sex. The ambiguous "hi" after a long drought of communication is the universal indicator that there's still gas in the tank.

Me
> 11:14am: heyo! i'm offended you didn't tell me earlier :)

Note the mimicry of lower case type to signify we are both so dumb that we're smart because we're above the idea that capital letters and proper grammar including run on sentences without commas are necessary to convey intelligence. It's a subtle way of saying that we get each other. The illiteracy in me respects the illiteracy in you.

Me
> 11:14am: of course let's catch up. where are you staying?

In journalism, that's called fact gathering. I hate myself for playing this game. It's a reflexive response. Flirting online is something our generation has 15 years of practice with. My earlier days on AOL Instant Messenger, the first mainstream chatroom, were rough because some things didn't digitally translate. My sarcasm has been strong since I was a young Padiwan, and it often made me sound like an asshole when I was trying to flirt. Sometimes it probably still does. Damnit.

Nikki

11:15am: i'm staying on a friend's couch somewhere in brooklyn. where are you

Nothing good comes over easy. Except sex. And eggs. Nikki and I met in college through Tree, a mutual friend whose name should double as an ancestry app. Tree was having a farm-themed party where he asked everyone to dress for a night of keg stands and line dancing. Keg stands are the thing where you do a handstand upside down on a keg while "friends" hold your feet up while you chug beer for as many seconds as you can. Line dancing is that thing where each song has a dance that all the women mysteriously know, and all the men try and act like they know because chicks love cowboys (despite being historically oppressive to women). By the end of the night, Nikki and I had danced with each other in both the Tim McGraw sense as well as the R. Kelly one. The line "it is on" went through my head multiple times that night.

Nikki

11:22am: ??

I lost my virginity when I was 20 to my girlfriend at the time, Lane. We were together for a year when she realized she couldn't wait anymore (she had lost hers at 15). She got on top of me and literally played just the tip. For those who have not played this game, there are no winners. In the most loving way, she later told me if I did not put out, she'd be out. I didn't realize how much Lane loved me until I thought about dating someone for a year without sex. Oral sex and denim grinding always have a special place in my heart, but life is short. In a related story, I didn't get drunk until I was 19. Lane was there too. These facts might correlate upon further review.

Nikki and I were back at Tree's house, fittingly called the Treehouse, the following night for a Finish The Keg party. FTK parties are intended for select people from the original party to drink until the prior night's keg is done. Worth noting that, despite our best efforts, we were not in a frat. Tree and I were friends because we alternated as our university's mascot, a giant fuzzy alligator. Some might argue that made us the opposite of frat boys. As the keg got tapped, Nikki gave me a squeeze on the hand and a familiar thought crept into my mind: it is on.

Down the hall in the spare bedroom, Nikki and I went in a controllably intoxicated, playfully sexual, and overly French makeout session. Nikki could kiss, and she had all the things you want in a woman: soft lips, body karate, college degree.

Me
   11:34am: i work in rockefeller center but i live in east village. Yall should swing by for lunch today? I cant do anything tonight but tomorrow night ill take yall out in my hood.

The definition of good sex lies in the body of the beholder. Nikki and I clicked because she was a masochist and I watched too much porn. Porn being the high production value stuff, not that weird titty-tying, leather mask wearing, step-on-my-balls stuff that I fear accidentally clicking on, only to leave my browser history and get discovered the next day. No no. Rough sex to me was, at that time, still simple. At 21, I was a two-year starter coming off the intercourse bench. I was not good at sex. Lucky for me, Nikki saddled up and rode herself to the Promised Land. One awkward tumble over and it was Hammer Time. As I approached the finish line, we both correctly said each others' names (not a given). In a heated exchange, she grabbed my thin gold necklace and accidentally yanked it off. The charm on the necklace was a cross. Britney Spears would call this a sign.

Nikki

11:37am: that sounds awesome! well make our way up there and just tell me when you're ready.

I grew up religious. Not the kind of religion that parents subdue their kids into, but actually by choice. I used prayer to cope with my family issues, social frustration, and constant erections. My best friend and I went to church together a lot. For a long time, we truly believed we were saving it for marriage. As a blue eyed, dark haired Armenian male, I was offered sex more than zero times in high school. The incredible power gained from withholding sex was temporarily mine. After that wall broke down, my self control went with it. Sex created this instant, addictive gratification. Sex was fun, but I wasn't completely oblivious to its imperfections or its way of pointing out mine. The cross Nikki had ripped from my neck was a gift I'd asked for on my 15th birthday, and I hadn't taken it off since. Unaware, she continued to pull me in as I literally and figuratively pulled out.

Me

11:38am: Okay, text me so we can communicate the old fashioned way...

I was doing something bad. Not bad in-the-court-of-law bad, bad in the technically-not-doing-anything-wrong bad. As Kanye says, "My heart ain't got nothing to do with my penis." Once you've hooked up with someone, they enter this sanctioned echelon of intimacy that even your closest friends don't get. There was a safety there. Sex was fun and having one-night stands would be even more empty without a post-mortem digital connection. Facebook stockpiles lovers, crushes, and exes, making them accessible long after they're gone. With social media as our memory card, we can justify romances by staying in touch. In the old days, if you had a one-night stand with someone in a different state a decade ago, it stayed a one-night stand. The ghosts of our sexual past never die, and it's easy to say "why not" when they want to come back from the grave for a Michael Jackson Thriller.

Nikki
12:46pm: hey just texted you, we're here.

I got her text. As much as I wanted to roll my eyes at the double confirmation, I was nervous. I hadn't seen a sex ghost in awhile. The excitement was chemical. Soft lips, body karate, college degree.

———

Not much had changed. The September sun laid itself across Nikki's cleavage in what can only be described as a generous display of goods. Her friend, standing there as the third wheel, wasted no time in asking about food. Like a true pair of Florida girls, they wanted BBQ. Like a true pair of Florida girls, they picked out the most touristy destination: Dallas BBQ. What is it about oversized, brightly colored cocktails that attracts people in their 20s? After two 32oz Tsumanis, I hugged the girls goodbye and briefly fantasized about a threesome.

2

SNAP, CRACKLE, POP

A ce Bar, East Village. About a 10-minute walk from my apartment, this lovely bar claims cheap drinks, Big Buck Hunter, and two unisex bathrooms. I generally recommend this bar to anyone who likes fun or sucks at dates and needs activities. I qualified for both. We walked into a familiar bar scene, but people in New York are on another level. Bars essentially don't close and designated drivers don't really exist, which means everyone is more tipsy than anywhere else. Nikki and I were there with this couple, Colby and Katie, for the night. After 20 minutes of playing darts, a game that should come with a timer, C and K did us the favor of winning. As that second beer went down, things started happening in my pants. I'd like to be that cocky guy that says things were happening in Nikki's pants too, but no man ever really knows what's happening in a woman's pants. Especially not me. Moments after saying goodbye to our soon-to-bone friends, we kissed. As her Angelina Jolie-esque lips mopped across mine, that magic moment happened. She slipped me the over-the-pants cock-squeeze (OTPCS).

Whoa.

One part whiskey, two parts beer. No bathroom breaks taken.

I'm running on a full tank with a woman in heels tapping on the sidewalk between avenues. The two things in New York City that expedite a man's walk home are women and restrooms. The two things that *delay* a woman's walk home are equally powerful: heels and pizza. Fortunately or unfortunately, neither of us were pizza-level drunk. I considered getting a slice to carb load for the six-floor walk-up that Nikki had no idea was in store. By the fourth floor, the words "what the fuck" escaped her mouth as we tried to kiss between the heavy breathing. There is a unique breed of panting that can only be experienced in the city's unique walk-up apartments. What I'll affectionately call a Phase-2 boner drained blood from my head as we entered my surprisingly clean apartment. When girls think they're going to get laid, they shave their legs and moisturize. When guys think they're going to get laid, they wash their balls and clean their apartment. I shouldn't generalize. *I* wash my balls and clean the apartment. Ball washing (manscaping implied) is an admittedly gross phrase but reflects a sense of courtesy for potential intimacy. The clean apartment shows a woman that I am responsible, organized, and, thus, would be a great person to disrobe with.

With the A/C on and primary layers of clothing off, I ran into the bathroom and peed for what felt like three minutes. I'd later find out in the hospital that this was quite possibly my best decision of the night. With an empty bladder, I scrambled to my phone to select a midnight soundtrack. In high school, I had a burned CD that was titled "Music to Bone By" for the hour-long make-out sessions I'd have. This included classics like Peaches and Cream by 112, Nice & Slow by Usher, Freek-A-Leak by Petey Pablo, and Closer by Nine Inch Nails. The mind of a 15-year-old virgin making a mixtape must have been something. On this particular night, I played the entire first album of The Weeknd. It takes exactly 27 seconds to realize that this album could have also very easily been called "Music to Bone By." As the bass drum kicked in, she wrapped her arms around me. Our bodies reflected back in the $10 mirror from Target. Nikki, in her maroon satin lingerie, pressed against me, wearing my generic gray boxer briefs. She hit me with one slow kiss on the right side of my neck. The tingle shoots down my body. A Phase-3, no looking back, hard-as-I-wanna-be boner arrives.

The body remembers in funny ways. Even though we hadn't seen each other in years, I instantly remembered the little intricacies of her sexuality. Touch is the greatest hidden talent of our memory. With little left to discover, we kick into second gear. I have home court advantage and pin Nikki to the wall. The weight of my 165-pound in-shape yet love-food-too-much body presses into her 115-pound, I-bet-other-girls-hate-you body. I keep one hand between her head and the wall (who says chivalry is dead?) and let the other hand slide south.

Discovering boundaries is an exciting part of foreplay at any age. Unless you know the other person's body, there is a lot of guessing going on. The argument can go both ways, but a guy can switch methods more easily. What I mean by that is, a girl usually has one way of stroking that she sticks to. Is she a speed demon? Double trouble? Palm licker? Reverse grip reach around? Downward dog? Kung Fu grip? Boob slapper? Tip ringer? Switch hitter? Most girls have a style they developed from a high school boyfriend. Blessed is the woman whose young love communicated the art of hand jobs. Cursed is the woman whose early love would've rather died than given constructive criticism.

Fortunately for women who never got the right training, vaginas easily get the job done. Guys, however, need years of training and a continued education to understand the clitoris. Instead of having one committed type of fingering for a girl, men have to engage in a series of trial and error. Is she north to south? East to west? X gon give it to ya? Flick of da wrist? Circles? Reverse circles? Double dribble? How about just the clit? Rent the runway. Bang Bang. Rock lobster. Middle finger in. Scout's honor? Three fingers in!? The list goes on and the shitty part is that it's often a changing combination that's difficult to predict. The good news for guys is that, so as long as we're in tune, women are good at indicating success. A subtle breath, literally the word 'yeah,' or her hand squeezing your hand all indicate success. These indicators are all necessary because we are dumb and all women are different.

Guys are all the same. The penis is not complicated. Unfortunately, we would still rather die than tell a woman she's been doing something wrong. Even when the woman directly asks what to do, it's a big risk. If someone cooks you a subpar dinner and asks you for your honest opinion, it still may be wise to smile and nod. Ipso fucto, we're both guessing until she's wet enough, he's hard enough, and the decision has been made whether or not to go to that damned old rodeo.

Somewhere before that happened, Nikki went down on me. What a gift. With every such gift comes the same thought: Am I going to reciprocate? I know, I know. I'm sorry! To be fair, women are not always open to cunnilingus (think body awareness). This is yet another complication in the art of pleasing a woman. As she's going down, we can barely concentrate because of all the other synapses going off. First and foremost, is she going to finish the job? If not, I've got to navigate these pleasure sensors. If so, we have to figure out what's going to get us there. Blow jobs are already tough. I like to enjoy them, but nobody wants them to go on for too long. Regardless of the quality, more thoughts flood in.

Why aren't you using your hands?

Wouldn't it be funny if you actually started to blow?

There's that noise again.

Should I stand up?

Should I hold your hair?

Does she think it's weird I'm trying to grab her boob?

Does it help me to grab a boob?

Why do girls put their hands on their hips in photos?

Boobs are awesome.

Does she know what a pearl necklace is?

I watch too much porn.

Hm. Porn.

When a girl says she likes giving head, is it safe to assume she's lying both to me and herself?
Gentle on the balls!
Honestly, I can stand if it's easier on your neck.
Why are you so good at this?
Why are you bad at this?
Should I feel bad about this?

I left my shining armor in Narnia and didn't reciprocate. We both understood it was a prep blow job, or blow task really, before sex. Much to my dismay, even women who are ready to do things are not a slip n' slide. One wrong blink between foreplay and intercourse and that well can dry up. With the understanding that she wasn't there to give head, I grabbed Nikki by the roots of her hair and pulled her face up towards mine, kissing her post BJ lips. Who said love was dead? At the age of 28, I was well aware of erection shelf life with alcohol present. With that in mind, I flipped her over and assumed the plank position. It's times like these I think about all those sit-ups I skipped. Maybe one day I'll be on top and a woman will marvel at my six pack. Then I think... is this a normal male thought? Maybe in Europe. I snap out of it. The express lanes are open and I'm entering the fast lane. I repeat, the car is accelerating into the fast lane. Whereas some guys are already thinking of how to tell their latest conqueror story, I'm busy honking the horn in my head. Here we go! I am on the freeway in the front seat, windows up.

BEEP BEEP MOTHER FUCKER!

Before I know it, sex is happening. All systems are on high alert. All hands are on deck. Those same hands search for purpose. For some men, the rest is history. Man has conquered and now must simply finish the race. For them, the hardest part is over. Nay I say, not I! In my need to forever be validated, I see physical intimacy as a chance to please someone else. Sex is an act that I, and many before, have been denied. I have an undeniable chip on my shoulder about sex. Being a good lover is my opportunity to say *Fuck You* to all the women that made me feel like shit, knowingly and unknowingly, long before I even had sex. Fuck you to the women that I tried to talk to at a bar, but got nervous because of my inability to flirt with strangers. Fuck you because athletes always got laid more than kids in the arts, even though it's not about quantity, of course...

Chip aside, sex was still happening and going rather well. Nikki and I didn't have the first time jitters with each other since we'd already been together, even if it was years ago. No matter what anyone says, the first bone is rarely the best. The best sex is fun sex, layered with pace and attention to detail for all involved. Best sex takes time. One-night stands are great, but also terrible. What I'm trying to say is that I am having sex and it's fun. She starts on top. This position is optimal when the man is righteously hard. The woman controls the pace and uses his yardstick as a .PDF (pussy depth finder, apologies for the p word). In my experience, women come more on top. In my experience, I don't. Everyone wins.

Sit up, pull her in, flip flop. Experts call this missionary, I think. Let me take a moment to give a public service announcement. From what I hear, this is where many men go wrong. Among the many instincts a man must subdue to be a good lover, the greatest is the urge to turn into a jack hammer. I have fallen victim to this move sometimes and will claim no sainthood. There are most certainly times that call for it, and sometimes a man just needs to cross the finish line. It is not our best trait, but it happens.

It boils down to self-control. That's what is required when a man is on top of a woman. To structure my self control, I revert to the 10 Count. The 10 Count came from an article I read long before my sheriff knew what a deputy was. The 10 Count came from my brother's high school subscription to Maxim Magazine, which my mother ordered so he would be a good lover when the time came. Good parenting or great parenting? Still unclear. The 10 Count was simple. Each round consisted of ten slow to moderate thrusts. In the first round, the guy goes in at 25% depth (see .PDF) nine times and 100% depth one time. That 100% depth is sometimes referred to as balls deep. Whoever comes up with these terms are logical, funny, and crass. For the second round, the guy dips his stick in the witches brew a quarter depth eight times and the last two he goes all the way in. This continues until one short thrust and nine full thrusts are happening. After this exercise in thrust control, both parties will have been primed for less than gentle sex. The 10 Count challenges a man's self control, core muscles, and lasting ability to stay significantly erect. Nikki and I made it about four rounds into the 10 Count before she grabbed my ass with both hands. Ever so delicately, the phrase "stop teasing" escapes through her teeth as she grabs my hips and says, "Fuck me." Mom would be so proud.

————

She is wet and I am hard. Both facts are good news. I'd love to say this is always the case, but that is obviously not true. The bad news is that my first sense of the end hit earlier than usual. We are two songs in, which by my calculations, is about six minutes since the doors have been breached. The pace car is catching up. Six minutes is not a respectable time for a guy to last. The sweet spot is between ten and fifteen minutes. At fifteen minutes, sexual activity enters the cardio zone, and anything past twenty minutes is a full on workout. If I stay on top at this point, the ship's going to blow anywhere from four minutes to five seconds. Do I think about saturated boobs and warm milk? No. I pull out and take my time rearranging into what scientists affectionately call "doggy style." Doggy style can't be the technical term, but I have no clue what it's actually called. Sideways T? Two by four? Hook and ladder? Half moon? Moon shiner? Whack a mole? Either way, I'm buying time. If the finish line was within inches, I would've gone down on her. Mid-sex oral occurs when the guy is either going soft and needs to discreetly bring himself back to life, or when he's too close to finishing and doesn't want to finish. Oral was not an option. She had already assumed the position and started to touch herself. I understand that some men might find this insulting, but I am not one of them. Strum away my little guitarrista! One team, one dream.

The moisture had mostly been sucked out of my mouth, but I attempted to silently lubricate myself without making a spitting noise. This is not attractive for a guy *or* a girl to do. Well, maybe that's not true. I can see people on both sides of the aisle being into that in a "you nasty Pun" way. Shout out to all the guys who watch too much porn (me) and are a little turned off when an "actress" does that obnoxious spitting thing. My lubricated WMD knocks on the door. Nikki's hand becomes the guide as she grabs my Colt .45 and moves it into the holster. She does this mainly to avoid any attempts, intended or accidental, at anal. The vagina has always been good to me, but some guys (and girls) are into anal. Pain for pleasure? I suppose.

Back on the bed, things are happening. Nikki is making sexy noises, indicating that things are going swell. To my delight, she thoroughly enjoys it from behind. Four songs in, Nikki and I hit our stride. I grab her hair by the roots and jerk her head back, leaning forward to kiss her sweaty neck.

Sex is fun. Sex is awesome. We are having sex.

A maniacal laugh escapes from both our lips. Pleasure takes the wheel and our forces combine in equal but opposite directions. Her lips tighten their hold, and I am in cruise control. It's the golden hour, that magical period of time when the woman is about to finish and the man is in no immediate danger of cutting her short.

"Right there, yeah, right there," she says.

"Yeah?"

"Yeah right there right there."

I quickly think what her name is.

"Yeah Nikki I want you to come."

"Yeah?"

Seriously though, please.

"Yeah"

"Oh fuck, fuck me Ross."

She proves she knows my name.

"Fuck Nikki!"

"Come with me, I want you to come with me!"

"Yeah?"

"Yes!"

My hands slide over her breasts and back, sinking into her torso. Her words flipped a switch in me and the finish line reveals itself. As terrible as this phrase is, she began to "fuck the shit out of me." Full strokes in and out. The total length of my ruler is being measured repeatedly. Sex is *awesome*! Nikki's right hand extends to the blank wall in front of her while her left hand desperately reaches for the curtain call.

"I'm coming fuck I'm coming come with me."

Bang.

Bang.

Bang.

*Pop.

My body arcs in pain. I turn up and to the left as blood shoots out the tip of my penis. My mouth releases a foreign noise of absolute and utter pain. Blood drips from the wall and onto the sheets. The tail end of that noise turns into a small yet omniscient phrase.

"Oh no."

3

IF IT WERE YOUR TOE

"What happened?" Nikki said on all fours.

The only response I could muster up was the sound of air being sucked through my clenched teeth. I laid on my side at the foot of the bed. The street lights shined through the window just enough to see the damage. Like a beached whale, my soldier rested helplessly on the sheets.

"Ross, what happened." Some questions don't need question marks.

She had no clue. I felt like I sent a mental signal to the entire universe, but somehow she missed it. Thousands of thoughts and scenarios fire through my mind, a different story for every person in my life. An imaginary text to everyone this would affect goes out to my friends, family, ex and current lovers. Nikki finally rolled onto her back. I carefully scoot off the bed and flick the light on. I look at her and deliver the news.

"I think I broke my penis." Those were the actual words I said in the most matter-of-fact way any man could. Looking back, the use of the word penis seemed rather proper for the situation. Looking down, the real situation continued to swell. If you take your pointer finger, point straight ahead, and then bend it a little to the left like a hook, that's a loose idea of what my tim tam looked like. Crooked.

"Are you serious?"

"Very." Panic set in on that word. I began to feel light headed. Instinct quickly combatted it.

"I'm calling 911," I said in the most pragmatic way with the phone already dialing, "and I'm feeling light headed." The disco stars were blinking in my vision as the internal sirens sounded in the distance. Nikki's hand covered her mouth to stop the 'Oh My God' phrase from continually spewing.

"You have my address in your phone, you have to buzz when they --," another voice entered my ear before I could finish.

"911, what is your emergency?" the operator interrupted my instructions with her infamous line.

———

People live their whole lives not dialing 911, and there's definitely a universal hesitancy to call for any non-dire situation. I'm the type that has trouble asking for help, even when I desperately need it. What if someone else was being shot at and I was tying up the line? My mind always finds time to have a counter point, regardless of the situation. Would the operator laugh when I verbalized my emergency? How would I say what I needed to say to avoid sounding like a prank call? Even if I knew the perfect thing to say, I've always been shy when it comes to talking to new people. When I was a kid, my parents would ask me to go into the store to return movies (back when people actually rented movies at stores), and I'd literally beg to not go alone. Interaction with strangers has never been easy for me, which my friends are always surprised to learn. Sociologists call it being an introverted extrovert, eye-roll implied.

"911, what is your emergency?" the operator's greeting repeated in my head.

"Hi. I think I'm going to need an ambulance. I believe I broke my penis." My medical tone and the use of the p-word discounted any possibility that this was a prank call. I have a recurring voice in my head, who is more like an urban translator, that delivers a dramatic rendition of my thoughts. My inner voice yelled, "My dick broke lady, send help!" The operator, who sounded like a Linda, understood that this was not a drill.

"I can't believe this," Nikki mumbled continuously in the background. It was a shared thought between her, Linda, and myself.

"Excuse me sir, can you repeat that?" Linda asked. I can't blame her. Audible words barely escaped my cottonmouth.

"I believe I broke my penis during intercourse just now," I reinforced.

"Okay, I understand. Are you in a safe place?" Linda asked, more out of habit than irony. For the first time, I started playing the 'what if' game. What if I was camping in the woods? What if we had pulled over on the highway? What if we were at some S&M sex party and I was hanging upside down, halfway into a glory hole? It's New York. Anything is possible and nothing can be written off. Linda has probably heard it all. Figure speech aside, I was in a safe place. The safest place, really. I was in my two bedroom, East Village apartment. East Village being synonymous for small and overvalued.

"Yes ma'am, I'm in my apartment in the East Village in Manhattan, New York."

Manhattan, New York was one of the dumber things I've said in my life, but Linda let it slide. Nikki sat against the wall, eyes pinballing around the room.

"Okay sir, what is your address?" I listened to her questions as I sat naked in my bright room. The lights seemed to get brighter and my head started to spin as the internal alarms tripped.

"Okay ma'am thank you."

———

My mom, God bless her, used to faint all the time. We grew up in Florida, where the heat hits everyone and the humidity forgives few. My mom loved to tan. She would lay out with her Australian Gold tanning oil and her oversized glass of water, perspiring in the sun as the ice rapidly melted near the top. The glass stayed full most of the time. I don't know why she didn't drink it, but by resisting the water I guess she was somehow sticking it to the man. In the 90s, that form of rebellion proved a woman's independence. I would know. I used to lay next to her in my hot pink shorts (it was Miami) while she played Madonna's Like A Prayer record. The aggregate amount of sun would catch up with her at random times and cause her to faint. My father, God bless him, had a strict. protocol to revive her.

- Step 1. Yell her name. And I mean yell. Sprinkle in a lot of hey's, hello's, stay with me's, and look at me's to reinforce the point. To this day, I've never seen a man yell the way he did when my mom would faint.
- Step 2. Gentle face slaps. This step meant she was not responding to the yelling. Her eyes were rolling back, similar to a mellow exorcism, and sweat was beading down her forehead.
- Step 3. Cold, wet rag. This was easy to remember because my dad would turn and yell at me to get this immediately after starting step 2. To this day, I've never had a man yell at me like he did when my mom would faint. Wipe cold rag over head and chest, then fold rag and lay across forehead.
- Step 4. Smelling salts. This step didn't exist until the faintings became habitual. Once my dad discovered those little packets, they could be found all over the house and even inside our car. One pinch on the black

dot in the center of these little white poppers and it
was on.

Each one of her fainting episodes acted as an event marker in
my life. Easter Service, First Presbyterian Church of Miami, 1990.
Orange Bowl, Nebraska vs Miami, 1992. Family Vacation, Norway
ride at Epcot Center, 1996. My father, God bless him, resolved
these unconscious spells accurately and efficiently. On one
particularly hot summer day, however, my dad wasn't home. My
mom and I tended the garden as Like a Prayer spun on the record
player. She always wanted a daughter so this was the type of
quality time we enjoyed.

"It is getting really hot, isn't it," she let out. Beep beep.
Emergency light flickers. I notice a glass of water inside our house,
sitting alone on the kitchen table.

"Yeah it's real hot Mommy." I was an agreeable child.

"Let's go inside." A few steps later she said, "I'm going to
faint," and promptly did. I was eleven years old and barely
through Confirmation, which is a loose Christian version of a bar
mitzvah. Instead of a party, my passage required a minor medical
procedure.

"Mommy?" She lies down.

"Get me that pillow for my head," and just like that, she passes
out. Jesus, take the wheel. Fuck fuck fuck fuck fuck fuck fuck fuck.

- Step 1. "MOMMY. MOMMY. HEY. MOMMY. HEY!
  LOOK AT ME!" I grab the glass of water sitting on the
  table with my two baby hands. "STAY WITH
  ME. HEY."
- Step 2. Splash! I throw the glass of water in her face.
- NO TIME FOR STEP 3!

"MOMMY!" I yell. She mumbles a response. Her eyes flicker
before the lights go out. Had I not seen this sequence of events
before, I would have assumed she died. Luckily, I remember that

sometimes she'll pass out cold for a couple seconds and that's okay.

SLAP! My adolescent palm catches her right in the face. I'm the man of the house now, and ain't nobody going to the hospital today.

"HEY. WAKE UP!" I go off script. "Can you hear me? LOOK AT ME." Her eyes flicker again. I consider the risk/reward of another slap. Fuck it.

SLAP! She blinks that where-am-I blink and I wait.

"Mommy, look at me. Hello?" She looks right at me, fully conscious. Mission accomplished. Cue Chris Brown, look at me now.

———

Nikki stared at me with an undeniably puzzled look.

"I'm feeling light headed, I might pass out. If I do, you have my address if they call my phone. Ambulance is on the way, you need to buzz them in right there. I'm going to sit down. Everything is going to be okay."

The people going through trauma usually have to comfort the bystanders. Her shock outweighed mine. I was in survival mode. Waddling across the room, I lowered my naked body onto the starchy Ikea futon.

"Can I get you anything?" Nikki asked helplessly. She found shorts on the floor and put them on. Her ass, aka the destroyer, looked great. Even at that moment, my mind actually had that thought.

"Yes, can you please get me a glass of cold water." Take a breath in. Breathe out. Breathe in. Breathe out. Do not pass out. Breathe. Survive.

"Can you grab me that wife beater?" I ask. I have a few of these terribly named tank tops in my drawer, but I'm not old enough or ethnic enough to wear them out in public. That takes a certain type of person. That said, wife beaters do make guys who work out marginally look like they have respectable shoulders. They also make guys look like mild sex offenders. Nikki obliged. She handed me the wife beater and, for the first time, she caught a glimpse of the beast.

"Oh my God," she gasped into a choked laugh of disbelief. I join her in observation and reach for my phone. For a brief moment, I leave my body as a male on the edge of collapse and become a millennial photographer. I steady the camera over the subject and take note. My penis looked like a tree with the base of 1,000 years and the height of ten that had been clubbed on the head. I snap one aerial photo of the carnage, briefly noticing that the manscaper had cut embarrassingly low. Adrenaline pumped through my body.

Wow.

Over the course of the next fifteen seconds, my brain synapses collapse over the following thoughts. My dick looks absurd. My dick looks huge. What am I going to tell Parker. Drink the water. I need shorts. Can I walk. Blood is still on the tip. I should be bleeding. Don't move. Touch it. Don't touch it. Why me. Insurance. What if my dick was always this big. It's crooked. I hope Nikki stays. I should send her home. This can't be happening. I can't feel anything. This is hilarious. Fuck. Me.

The door buzzes. Nikki checks her watery eyes in the mirror. She had hid her tears of hysteria up to that point. As the heavy footsteps of the medics climbed the crimson stairwell, I prepared my first explanation of many. A deep voice boomed through the pint-sized foyer.

"Hello ma'am, I'm Joe. How are you?" I saw them before they saw me. Dispatch sent me two men who can only be described as Jersey Shore alternates. One large man and one small man arrived from what was either a gym or a hair salon. Linda knew she needed to send men who understood the stakes of my predickament. With a pair of basketball shorts draped over my boomstick, I looked up at the two Italian bodybuilders and smiled.

"I'm sure you guys see a lotta shit, but I think this one might be up there for a couple weeks." These guys looked like the types that would start a fight if someone accidentally bumped into them, but they couldn't have been kinder from the moment they walked in. They cowered over me with a couple basic questions about what happened and eventually asked to take a look. Like an amateur magician, I gently lifted the University of Florida basketball shorts to reveal the rabbit had disappeared from inside the hat. Only, the rabbit had not disappeared, it had doubled in weight and mass.

Medics see unthinkable gore, and it can be unnerving how passive they are with it. It's one thing for a friend to see something twisted and react with no regard. It's another thing to watch a medical professional see an injury and gently mouth the word "fuck." It was bad. I knew it was bad. I actually appreciated their honesty and it quickly validated their humanity.

"I know bro, I know." Bros around other bros have a multiplier effect. While I'm truly not a bro, I adapt quickly to the personalities around me. It's a survival tactic to fit in when you want people to like you. It's also a sign that I grew up in the theatre.

"Alright can you walk?"

Yes.

"We can take you down in a stretcher, but that might be harder for you." I am of the theatre, but I am not theatrical. I pulled my elastic blue shorts over each of my three legs with the help of everyone in the room. There's a wonderful Bill Murray movie, *What About Bob*, where Murray's character has a simple mantra for overcoming problems. He repeats the phrase "baby steps." Baby steps out of the office. Baby steps down the hall. Baby steps to the car. Looking at the ten feet between the door and me, I literally and figuratively enlisted this mantra.

After flights of baby steps, we arrived outside to find the ambulance waiting. With a handful of steps left to get in the back, I paused to ask a question. The paramedic closest to me turned rather quickly, despite the circumference of his torso, as I delivered my ponderance.

"Do you think I should take a taxi to the hospital?" I asked. It's hard to believe how rational my mind was being given the circumstance, but I have always been hyper aware of the cost of healthcare.

––––––

When the economy crashed, my dad lost his job in pharmaceutical sales. He immigrated to the US to attend Harvard with little to his name, taking only math classes when he arrived so he had time to learn English (his third language). Upon becoming unemployed, he started hustling his old clients for consulting work and would do anything to support the family. Needless to say, we all made budget cuts. Of those cuts, we downgraded our insurance from premium to catastrophic. Catastrophic insurance meant, as my mom told me, "If you're going to get hit by a car, make sure it's a bus."

Throughout all of high school, I only put myself in danger if I thought my insurance would cover it. No backflips into the pool. No half pipe at the skateparks. No armwrestling. No unsupervised cooking. And no contact sports. The usual stuff. Luckily, the uber cool combination of theater and band naturally kept me out of harm's way. My mom knew that any routine visit to the doctor could cost hundreds of dollars, and any small visit to the hospital wouldn't hit our deductible. I learned at an early age the obscene, uncapped cost of healthcare.

If you're going to get hit by a car, make sure it's a bus.

––––––

Joe the medic looked at me and fielded my financial concern.

"Look bro," he started, unwavering from our bro status, "it's ultimately your choice." I calculated costs in my head while he explained the most obvious answer ever.

"We're going to get you where you need to be faster and safer than anyone else. Do you have insurance?" This question haunted me, even though my employer supplied a generous health care package.

"Yeah, Blue Cross Blue Shield," I confirmed. Nikki, still miraculously there, asked if she should hail a taxi. In line with typical human behavior, the second I got offered what I had proposed, I immediately went for the opposite. Joe and his double hoisted me up into the bed of the ambulance.

"You had me worried for a second," he said climbing in and closing the door. "If it were your toe, I'd say maybe. But this ain't your toe." His grammar were wrong, but he was right. Verified by its swelling size, it was not my toe. The driver made a phone call and relayed that we were going to pass the closest hospital for a better one, Weill Cornell Medical Center. This decision, unbeknownst to me at the time, saved my strife. The sirens briefly sounded off as we sped towards the Upper East Side.

4
DAD, ED, AND EDIE

F un fact. The ER is also known as the ED, or emergency department. These late night workers see it all, and tonight they were getting a show. The hospital escort greeted me with a curious smile. She led me down the infinite hallway as the entire staff stood by watching. Like a misplaced prom queen, I smiled and nodded at the people we passed. My glossy eyes glistened in the fluorescence light.

I've often felt like I am an observer in my own life. When these odd things happens to me, which they often do, I think... hmm, that would happen to Ross. This allows me to laugh at life's ridiculousness in times like these. This particular time was no exception. Trailing behind me, Nikki was having a less majestic experience. This poor woman, in all her guilt, walked with the weight of the world on her shoulders. While I was the waving prom queen, she was enduring shaming looks from the crowd. While people smiled at me, they shook their heads at her. She was taking the longest, slowest, most well lit walk of shame known to date.

The clock's arm moved past 1am.

On the gurney in front of me lay a blue and white assless mumu. Nikki, God bless her, and the ED attendant carefully undressed me. The attendant marked the third stranger that had seen me naked in the past hour. With my chic mumu tied on, I carefully rolled onto the gurney. After the five minutes that took to accomplish, an attractive brunette nurse came in the door. She rolled in with a tray of needles and a beautifully devilish smile, or at least that's how I saw it.

"Ross?" she asked in her deep Southern accent.

"That's me!"

"I'm Edie, I'll be one of your nurses."

"Edie, the legend."

"Yes, that's me," she proclaimed, mimicking my greeting.

"How are you feeling?"

People stop asking "How are you doing" and start asking "How are you feeling?" when you've had medical issues.

"On top of the world." I would use this answer every time someone new would ask. This playful sarcasm warmed up the medical staff for the ironic tone and barrage of blue humor that was coming their way.

"Oh well that's good," she laughed, masking the sound of needles coming out of their sterile, plastic wrap. *Fuck needles*, I thought, in unison with everyone in hospitals everywhere. If a person ever says they don't mind needles, run the other way. Some might argue that people get used to needles. Wrong. In my freshman year of high school, I volunteered at the Disney Cancer Institute in Orlando. By now it should be apparent that my skill set has never lent itself much to the sciences, but they accepted me because my book-smart brother had volunteered there years before. The doctor I shadowed, Dr. Vain, specialized in children's Leukemia and routinely administered spinal taps on kids much younger than me. A spinal tap is a medical procedure where the doctor takes a large needle and punctures the patient's lumbar to collect cerebrospinal fluid, or CSF. CSF surrounds the brain and spinal cord and can diagnose a myriad of issues including cancer. The long needle used to extract the fluid looked like the ones they used in X-Men to inject Wolverine with Adamantium. 'Needleless' to say, the procedures weren't for weak stomachs. My job was to play with the kids and make them smile so they would have a friend in the room during this brutal procedure. Dr. Vain asked me to sit in a chair the first time I was in the room.

"Even people with a tough stomach get queasy," he told me as I briefly attempted to man up. The kid lay on his back, thankfully looking towards his mother, as the needle pierced the bone. *Crack.* My mouth went dry and my eyes squinted. I didn't pass out, but I came damn close. The lumbar puncture sounded like two rocks knocking into each other and turning. This kid, four years my junior, had more heart than I could have ever imagined when we were playing with action figures twenty minutes before.

———

"It could always be worse," I said after Edie commented on my surprisingly positive attitude. The needle butterflied into my arm injected a cool liquid. The taste on my tongue went from dry to metallic. Morphine, the type of drug reserved for TV dramas, flooded my system.

"Eight milligrams," Edie told me. Apparently, I asked. With little notice, Edie disappeared and Nikki held my hand. She contained her hysteria as I rambled off about how I felt funny. I didn't do drugs growing up, and I enjoy being an adult with a lot of firsts yet to be ticked. As a result, I endlessly verbalize my experience to amuse people that went through similar ones a decade or so earlier.

"Ross?"

"That's me!" I instinctively react.

"My name is Peter," he said as my mind scrambled to make a joke about his name.

"Of course it is." I point to the perpetrator, "This is Nikki, my bodyguard." He introduced himself and acknowledged her kindness in being present.

"How are you feeling?"

"On top of the world baby!"

He laughed a bit and acknowledged the importance of a good attitude. Nurse Peter emitted a warmth that made me immediately comfortable, which I needed despite the banter. Peter posed a lot of questions to Nikki and me. "Were you drinking?" was my favorite. This seemingly rhetorical question was always followed by "how many," which no one knows how to answer properly. The questions Peter asked made me think how it happened was rather boring. He asked me to walk through the night, which I did. Then he asked Nikki to walk through the night from her perspective. She walked through the same position sequence and, to my delight, added that she experienced an orgasm right before it happened. I mentally fist bumped myself as though I had something to do with it.

"Interesting," Nurse Peter noted. "Did you ever experience any emissions from your Skene's gland during intercourse?" Nikki and I exchange looks to confirm neither of us know what sex robot language he's speaking.

"Female ejaculation," he clarified. This awkward moment continued for another second until Nikki giggled out.

"Oh, like, am I a squirter?" I suppose a doctor's instinct is to use proper medical terminology for as long as possible until she or he returns to dumb-dumb civilian phrases. Nikki was not a squirter. I have mixed feelings about squirters. On one hand, the male gets physical affirmation that he is actually doing something right. On the other hand, what a fucking mess. I realize that the same can be said about a guy unloading on any person, place, or thing he can find, but we are, at our core, basic cavemen entertained by our own idiocracy.

Part of the idiocracy is that men want to bone in as many different places as possible. A trait that I believe was set in motion when we read *Oh the Places You Will Go*, a Dr. Seuss book and the most predictable gift for a high school graduation. Being on morphine, a quite wonderful drug, my mind wandered off to all the places I've had sexual encounters. These included: a bed, a boat, a car, a van, an SUV, the Atlantic Ocean, the Pacific Ocean, a Costa Rican shower (not safe), a Portuguese bathroom, the Holiday Inn, a Holiday Inn Express, a tent, the Ramada Inn, a phone booth, a driveway in Orlando, the Haunted Mansion Ride at Disney, a movie theatre (it was a Claire Danes movie), backstage of a Shakespeare show, on a balcony, a costume shop, an unstable treehouse, poolside, in a pool, the common room of a nice apartment building, a tiki hut, and an overnight bus in Spain. That being said, I had a relatively normal sex life. I often wonder if I have a crazy fetish waiting to be unlocked. Maybe that thing isn't feet or leather or S&M or autoerotic asphyxiation or role play or dirty talk or tandem. Maybe it's location. Morphine revelations, I suppose.

"When was the last time you urinated?" Nurse Pete asked.

"Um, right when I got back to the apartment," I replied.

"Okay, let's stand you up and see if you can go right now." Nurse Peter hoisted me up as I swung my three legs over the bed. He handed me a large red jug that looked more fit for spare gasoline than urine samples. With a small audience, a shy bladder, and a half lifted mumu, I tightened my abdomen and tried to fill the jug. Ten long seconds go by and nothing moves. No worries, I've been here before. For all the times in a public bathroom where the guy chooses the adjacent one urinal to mine, or the long lines at a bar or sports game where there's pressure to keep the line moving, I could do this. I stood there, crouched over the gasoline can, while Peter and Nikki silently encouraged me. They looked right at me, as more walls of privacy tumbled down.

Come on, damnit! I thought. *You can do this.* Except, I couldn't do this. I could not physically urinate. I paused before looking up at their disenfranchised faces. For the first time in this whole ordeal, I felt helpless.

"I can't," I told them, deflated. Who we are in these little moments of mortality were so hard to define. My mind immediately dropped into a depression of discouraging thought. Nurse Peter gently took the jug back and left the room. The next 15 minutes took a little longer than usual. The hospital buzz settled and the details of the room blurred. Nikki had gone for a walk, which I had encouraged. I needed time alone with my destitute self.

What have I done.

   Why is this happening to me.

   I literally have the worst fucking luck in the world.

   What happens if I can't pee? Like, what does that mean?

The mind can be a terrible thing when left to itself. After the existential thoughts faded, my subconscious kicked in. She had been there the whole time. Behind every rational thought about the whole situation, she crept in. She being an actual girl, not my subconscious. Parker Fields was no ordinary girl. She was a fucking woman. Smart, independent, kind, and classy. The later of which was inflated by her posh English accent. I met Parker on a weekend in upstate New York where the group had no cell service and didn't talk about work. I didn't know what she did or barely who she was, but I hadn't felt the urge to take a girl on a proper date in a long time. Parker's eyes looked like the crystallized color reserved for anime characters. She had other features, but, for me, a certain hue of blue eyes trumps everything else. Women can squat their way to an ass, buy themselves a nice pair of boobs, and poke themselves into youth, but eyes remain the same. That's why when it comes to profile pictures, I never trust a girl in sunglasses.

I was going to tell Parker what had happened. Of course I was going to tell her. What I didn't know was how or when I would tell her. How and when would I tell the world, really. There was that whole job thing. Then there was that whole family and friends thing. At this point, the extent of the damage hadn't been clarified.

All I knew was that the clock had surpassed 2am, and a new person in scrubs waltzed into my room.

"Ross?"

"That's me!"

"I'm Traci. How are you feeling?" Traci, who may or may not have been a nurse, was attractive. Her complexity was a stunning mix of the world, and her accent had some Irish in it but was hard to peg. Genetic diversity is a beautiful thing that was really working for my impotent eyes. Also, are scrubs supposed to be sexy? I don't think they are, but then sometimes the mystery of banality has a reverse effect.

"Top of the world ya know?" I replied.

"That's good," she smiled out. "The doctor is almost ready to run a couple tests and take some x-rays. I'm going to take you to the exam room."

Traci unhinged my mobile bed and began the slow process of transporting me to the next room. She drove my gurney like a student learning to drive a stick shift. She powered through the bumps and compensated turns by accepting minor scratches along the way. My feet lay over the edge like bumpers waiting to push off any obstacles in the way.

"Is the art this bad throughout the whole hospital?" I asked. The framed painting of faded flowers clung to the walls with justified insecurity. They begged for vibrance. They had likely been acquired for free, which is understandable I guess. If Paul Gauguin had a child with a desaturated paint palette, these paintings would have been the result. Traci enlightened me with her optimism.

"I kind of like it," she philosophized. "If the art in here stood out, everyone would be cluttering the halls." She had a point, I think. My feet knocked into something every other turn, and I almost said something snarky, but I was still her helpless passenger. It's for this reason, I never understand people that are rude to their taxi drivers before they get to their destination.

"Ross?"

"Yes that's me."

"I'm Dr. Wang," This was her actual name. Well played, Universe.

"We're going to run a couple tests on you to try and figure out exactly where the tear is."

A cystoscopy. That was the procedure. A cystoscopy, or a cysto as the locals call it, involves a thin tube with a camera on it going into the tip of a penis. Except it wasn't a penis, it was my penis. The cysto allows the doctor to find out exactly where the damage is. That way the doctor knows what they're getting into before the operating room, or OR. The dimly lit x-ray room felt like a club, designed to keep my sight hidden from the truth of my surroundings. One giant machine sat in the middle with one giant robot arm hovering over one small table. A shielded booth in the corner protected the techs from radiation, but they clearly wanted to take a look. As I transferred beds, I spotted the instrument of doom that awaited entry into my urethra. The word "fuck" repeated in my head followed by a "me," "this," or "that" in rapid succession. The cystoscope, or instrument of doom, looked like a miniature whip with a blood pressure pump as a handle. As I lay on the thin, sterile wax paper, I began to think about that morphine drip. I began to think about something going in my penis instead of out. The out hole was becoming an in hole. The exit was becoming an entrance. Is this what anal is like?

"Dr. Wang?" I mumbled out. My dry voice struggled to make words, but I had to ask the obvious question. "Should I have more morphine, maybe, before you do this tube thing?"

"We'll give you some numbing gel, but you'll be fine. This procedure should take 60 seconds at most." Dr. Wang was a liar. I didn't know she was a liar or that she was lying at that very moment, but, then again, neither did she. I glanced over to the technicians standing in their blue scrubs. They felt for me. I don't know why that gave me comfort, but they see their fair share and still peered over with visible sympathy across their faces. The cold room made me shiver a bit as I tried to man up, in the traditional sense. The time had come. Dr. Wang gently rolled me onto my side, and I peered over to catch her name badge. I couldn't believe her last name was actually Wang, yet there it was. Often times life cracks jokes in ways a writer would be fired for, but her name tag didn't lie.

The honorable Dr. Wang delicately held my swollen thumb as she mumbled medical words to her tech, Gary. Another assistant, Carrie, appeared with the black snake camera and relayed that she was ready for insertion. I hope one day a nerd uses this line on a girl before losing his virginity.

"Okay here we go and --"

Faaaaaahhhhhhhhhkaaasaaan.

Breathe in. Breathe in. Breathe in.

"You doing okay?" Dr. Can't-Believe-It's-Wang asked. I gripped the table and chewed air in small yet efficient bites. Sixty seconds -- don't be a little bitch! I could feel the damn thing inside of me, and looking at the freak show I'd become from the waist down didn't help. I had to look away despite my masochistic tendencies.

"Yeah good," I squeaked. At that moment, I thought of Nazi Germany. I thought of their experimental doctors and the tests they'd run on Jewish people in the camps. I thought of one test in particular I'd read about where they'd stick glass rods in the men's soft dicks and then stimulate them to get hard so it'd shatter inside them. WHAT THE FUCK. What a fucking bunch of shitheads. I thought about Heaven and Hell. In that moment, I wanted Hell to exist for the sole purpose of torching the dicks of those Nazi doctors and scientists for eternity.

Breathe in. Breathe out. Breathe in. Breathe out.

Years earlier, I had learned about meditating. I'm still not sure how I feel about the commercialization of it, but the practice has always had its personal benefits. For now, it kept the pain at bay and my mind off the clock. Sixty seconds right? Dr. Wang fumbled around and still hadn't found what she was looking for. Cue U2 and my immediate regret for asking if I should have more morphine instead of simply requesting it. The doctor relayed commands back at Gary and Carrie, both failing at their poker face, to take the x-rays. I didn't know what they were saying to each other because I focused on not moving. The cystoscope, aka black mamba, went in deeper. It felt not great. My eyes opened and closed, unsure as to which was better. Carrie, unable to fully know the pros and cons of a cock, stayed glued to the equipment. Gary's face winced.

I see you, Gary. *I SEE YOU BRO.*

"Dr. Wang, should I prep the dye?" asked Carrie, who was obviously named for her exorcisms. The sixty seconds had to be up by now, and there was still something inside of me.

"Yes, let's see if that shows up. Ross, hang in there, we're going to insert a dye and see if --" I gave zero fucks what she was saying. I heard every word and knew my only option was to agree.

"How are you doing?" she asked again.

Go fuck yourself, lady. I knew she was there to help me so I kept that phrase in my head.

"Top of the world," I joked. She laughed. I gave a little fake laugh to acknowledge that it was indeed a joke, and it was okay to laugh. Huge mistake. Laughing tightened my dick muscle around the black mamba-scope, sending a shock of pain into my intestine.

More morphine please! I knew it was too late, so I kept that phrase in my head as well. Breath in. Breath out.

I started to sing a song in my head. Will You Be There by Michael Jackson. This song was best known as the theme song from the movie *Free Willy*. Will You Be There was my favorite Michael Jackson song, and the irony was not lost on me that *Free Willy* was about a giant whale escaping from captivity. Apparently, my subconscious does blue humor even when I'm preoccupied. A flush of cool tingles shot through my body. Dr. Wang had injected a dye through a new instrument that I hadn't noticed. I guess the numbing gel worked better than I thought. The hovering x-ray machine took a couple pictures as my body froze in place.

"Okay Ross," my good friend Dr. Wang said as she removed her blue surgical gloves, "there is some blockage in your urethra, which is why we took the x-rays. I'm going to review them soon, but let's get you up. Are you feeling alright?"

"Never been better." I knew she was helping, so I tried to combat my internal negativity with external positivity. I am therefore I think. Right? Gary and Carrie assisted me back to my transport vehicle. Purple dye lingered on the tip of my penis. It looked wasted off of Kool-Aid on a hot summer day in the Tennessee Williams sort of way. Traci didn't care. She had been waiting to cart me back to my room, bad British driving skills and all.

"How did it go, love?" The words chirped out of her sweet mouth.

"Wonderfully. I could've used some more morphine, that's for sure."

"Did you ask?"

"I asked if I should just brave it out or if I'd need more."

"Never ask a doctor that. They always want you to brave it out, otherwise they have to wait for the medicine to settle, and doctors aren't ones to queue." Lesson learned.

Back in the well-lit ER room, Nikki asked Dr. Wang questions that she didn't want to hear the answers to. I didn't really care to tell her, but conversation helped pass the time and the absurd reality of the situation. As much as I appreciated Nikki's presence, she would leave soon, and I had to prepare for the people who actually existed full time in my life.

———

I had only been in the emergency room on one other occasion, and my dad stood beside me the whole time. It was a hot October day in Miami, my city of birth. I was a mere six years old. My dad took trips to the La Vaquita, a local gas station with a cow on the sign, whenever our 1985 Honda Accord needed a fill. For most of my life, I would sit in the car as my dad filled it up. During the past couple of trips to La Vaquita, he let me hold the pump with him.

His giant hand covered my baby hand with security and confidence. Since kids always think they're older than they are, I thought the time had come for me to pump it solo.

"Can I pump the gas by myself, Daddy?" Combining both confidence and cuteness in my ask.

"Do you think you're ready?" he baited.

"Yeah, I can do it."

"Okay, I'll start with you and then let go."

"Okay got it."

We stepped out of the bronze, four-door sedan and walked to the pump. Back in those simpler days, people paid by walking inside the station and having actual human interaction with the cashier. My dad strolled in to see the cashier and owner, Taline. My dad could make friends with anyone, and our local gas station owner was no exception. I stood by the car studying the scene and hyping myself up. I have always been a baby, scared of everything from big thrills to little bugs. I had sensitive feet and I couldn't eat spicy food. I knew my shortcomings, but this time I stood with both feet ready to move forward into manhood.

"On pump number four please," my dad said, handing Taline a twenty dollar bill from the wad of cash that only dads carry. I watched him walk out of La Vaquita towards the man I was about to become. The wind lifted my chin as my eyes squinted in the morning sun. Before I knew it, my dad hit the yellow 87 octane button on the kiosk and unhooked the valve. He took my hand and put it on the rubbery black handle. It was fucking on.

"Hold on to it very tight," he said with absolution. How hard could this be? Put the hose in the hole and don't let go. I would be asking myself similar questions years later. For now, my dad encased my baby hand in his as the metal tip went into the gas tank. We squeezed the handle and I felt the gas flow. The valve resisted, but we pushed together. I knew I could do this.

"Ok let go Daddy," I declared with confidence in my high pitched baby voice.

"Are you holding on tight?"

"Yeah Daddy I am, let go I got it." I tightened my grip on the head of the hissing python. My dad let go with caution and took a step back. The rumble of the hose shook my baby hands, now solely responsible for our future. In an instant, the Miami heat grease the inside of my baby palms. Uh oh. Exactly two seconds later, the nozzle came loose and all hell broke with it. Gas spewed out as the hose whipped into my face. I screamed. My dad, in all his dad-strength quickness, darted in to tame the outpour of gasoline. The snake hit the ground, gasoline still oozing from its demon mouth. I felt the burn take hold of my body. Most kids endure their first bout with pain from a broken bone or a twisted ankle. I, of course, experienced mine through liquid fire.

My dad sent a string of Armenian curse words to the sky as he scooped me into his arms. Within moments he bursted through front door of the gas station.

"Call 911, there's gas in his eye. Where is the bathroom?" My dad, in all his dad strength, had already found it.

"IN MY EYES, DADDY MY EYES ARE BURNING, DADDY," I yelled. I wailed, really. The more I opened my eyes, the more the gasoline oxygenated and the more I wanted to die. "IT BURNS DADDY I WANT TO DIE." I screamed those words into my dad's face as he flushed my eyes and body with water. He used the tiny bathroom sink like a basin, blessing me with copious amounts of water until help arrived. My shirt was off and a rag scrubbed my body.

"I'M SORRY DADDY IT BURNS, ALL IN MY EYES," I proclaimed. The sting was bad. My dad must have felt worse, holding his dramatic son as he screamed "I want to die." I wasn't being theatrical either. Pain sticks with you, and I remember feeling this invisible burn take my body over like it was yesterday. Before I knew it, there were two giant, yellow-coated firemen in the door. They had arrived dressed as though I was indeed on fire, and they were ready to put me out. My next memory of that scene was laying on a hospital bed, looking at a bag of clear liquid drip, dropping one by one.

Back in the ED, I looked around the quiet room. Two fluorescent lights, an empty chair, and a bag of fluid dripping each drop one by one. History repeats itself, and I was watching the reruns as the clock moved past 3:30am. My eyes finally gave in as I drifted off into a helpless sleep.

5

I JUST CALLED TO SAY

Reception in the room wavered. My phone battery dips to 65%. Who do I tell? My brother makes sense, but he lives in a different time zone. My parents, well -- no. I open the mail app on my phone and begin typing to my roommate.

Date: Fri, Sep 26 at 6:38 AM

Subject: Greys anatomy

In the adventures of my life, this one is up there. Long story short I essentially tore a penis muscle and fractured my urethra having sex with that girl. The first girl since Parker, of course so karma? Idk. Anyways, I'm going to have surgery soon...rather it'll be done when you're up probably, but wanted to let you know. Nikki, the girl, has your number and was here most of the night. Hoping they can fix everything, but there's a chance they can't...which would suck. This is definitely not going to be the story I tell pretty much anyone so don't Instagram it, and hang tight til I make something up. I hopefully won't need any help but there's a shot I may need you. Other than that in good spirits, definitely giving everyone at the hospital a good story.

There are certain emails that give my gut an extra punch once I click the send button. This was one of them. My penis was now out in the universe. I drafted another email to my brother and had little hesitation in hitting send. As I clicked the compose button for a new email, my chest sank. I've dated five women in my life. Actually, I've dated three if I'm not counting my middle school girlfriend (who told me during the VMA's that she made out with this guy Michael on the swim team and wanted to break up with me. So Mike, if you're out there, FUCK YOU BUDDY). I also don't count this girl in college that told everyone she was my girlfriend to the point that I actually started agreeing. Scientists call this dating by submission. All women I dated had something in common. I never actually asked any of them out, which isn't to say I'm some prince that can only be courted. My girlfriends were all friends that parlayed into relationships. We always began as friends, and once our tongues met we'd soon after be holding hands. This was the path I was on with Parker.

"Three things I don't know about Parker," I said. This is something I do to get to know people while also avoiding awkward pauses, weather talk, and hearing about someone's job.

"What?" she said, obviously to buy time. Raising my three fingers in the air (pinky, index, middle), I silently encouraged her.

"I don't know. You go!"

"Nope, you first."

"Ummm, I don't know!"

"Of course you do -- ONE."

We were flirting.

"I can ride a unicycle," she blurted out.

"Amazing. TWO." I love this game.

"Ummm."

"Can be literally anything."

"I've never seen Star Wars, Indiana Jones, or The Matrix."

"Unclear if that's even possible, but yes... three?" When I play this game, I don't ask questions until the end.

"Oh gosh I don't know," she was laughing at the thought of all the parts of her she wasn't ready to tell me, but also at the silliness of it all.

"Yeah c'mon give me something good."

"Um, ok wow. In high school, my nickname on the soccer team was Nips, which is short for Nipples."

Parker was different. I don't mean different in the romantic sense either. She was gravitational. Gravity in a mate can vary physically, and to describe her physical attributes may not convey how she made me feel. Her eyes pulled me in from the first moment I met her. One month after we met, we had spent a lot of time together. We also spent a lot of time apart, mixed up in our own journey. New York relationships are fleeting and replaceable. Time apart in the city weakens that security with a force unmatched by any other city.

"What do you want?" she asked me. An insanely high number of guys would say 'sex' in their head. Quite honestly, I do too most of the time. Steak, massages, world peace, and an airline buddy pass float as potential answers as well. But for the first time, I blurted out something that I meant.

"I want you to be my girlfriend."

———

Date: Fri, Sep 26 at 7:21 AM

Subject: Little lion man

This is unfair, especially since I said I'd stay out of your headspace. But I'm not going to hide or delay what just happened. Long story short I essentially tore a penis muscle and fractured my urethra having sex with a former college hookup who randomly was in town tonight. The first and only girl since you, of course so, karma? I don't know. I'm going to have surgery soon, been in the hospital all night... but needless to say it's not fun. This isn't going to be the story I tell anyone so don't Instagram it please. I wish we didn't give each other space, and even though I've been waiting for you to tell me it's not going to work (again), this is a dumb reason that makes it easy for you to push me away.

I'm not sure what mental state I'll be in in the coming days but there will probably be a lot of painkillers, so I didn't want to wait and be loopy when I told you.

I really wanted you to be my girlfriend, and this sucks. I'm really sorry. I would've rather this be with you, in a very weird, sick and twisted way. Ok, that's all I got. They're going to put me under in an hour probably.

Send.

Blank pages flipped through my brain for an hour. We are all so dumb. I am so dumb. For the next hour, I thought about my penis. This is not uncommon for a guy, but they were not the usual thoughts. I thought about Parker. I thought about her reaction to reading my email and how stupid it was that, as a human, she'd have to write anymore than "okay" in response. Did I cheat? What do you do if someone cheats? Is it black and white? How many times do you hear about a friend of a friend's relationship that stayed together anyway. If everything happens for a reason, is that my excuse? I wouldn't have done this if the universe wanted us to be together. We have the ability to justify anything, and we'll believe our own bullshit if we say it enough. Laying on my gurney, I contemplate the universe, fate versus destiny, free will, and freeing Willy.

———

My new driver knocked at the door. The early morning hospital worker arrived, stoned out of his mind.

"Hey buddy, good morning man," the young man repetitively said. "How are you feeling?" His name tag read Mitch. Fitting.

"Top of the world, Mitch. What's the good news?"

Before I knew it he was driving me through the halls. Driver's ed doesn't teach gurney turns, and Mitch was living proof you didn't need a license in these manila hallways. With little room to readjust, my feet once again clipped doors and handle bars. I counted three apologies in between his stoned commentary about none other than the hospital art. Did they plan this?

"Look at this one," he began. "Do you think we should just have wallflowers instead of these old paintings? I have a buddy who is doing that for this bar in Queens." The paintings were of flowers. He was the type to answer the question in the same breath he was asking it. He must have a lot of one way conversations in this job. Because I was also a little high, I kind of enjoyed his three minute conversation about subpar hospital art, hospital art dealers, and his days as an Art Institute dropout. I wonder what Mitch and Traci talk about in the break room. As my feet knocked into the wall on another turn, we arrived at the door of the operating room.

"Doctor Seems will take you from here brother, take it easy man." The double use of bro terms is a sure sign of being baked. Seems was short for Seema. Dr. Seema, the anesthesiologist, smiled at me to signify she was not in the same state of mind, but fully prepared to take me to the next level.

"How are you feeling?"

Life, repeating itself once again...

"Top of the world."

"That's wonderful," she laughed with her belly as any sedation doctor would on TV. A barrage of nurses floated over me as the fluorescent lights began to blind me. Each new player appeared with an introduction and some sort of cutlery. Jokes happen in the OR all the time, and I guess the hilarity of my situation and attitude gave them license to let them roll before I was completely out.

"What's your favorite drink?" Dr. Seema asked.

"Depends where I am. Umm, whiskey rocks with orange zest seems about right now."

"It's never too early for a nice whiskey. I'm going to make you a nice cocktail. Think of the smoothest whiskey, that's what you're getting." I was unsure what I was hearing, but subtle references to cocktail drugs both scared and relaxed me. If someone's got a direct line into your veins, the move isn't to go against their sense of humor.

"Dr. Herm is here." With a calming hand, the operating doctor floated above the crown of my head and put his larger, soothing hands on my shoulders.

"Hi Ross, I'm Dr. Herm," he gently said. "You're young and healthy, and we're going to take care of you. You're going to be just fine." With those words, I sank into myself and the lights faded to black. Goodnight and Godspeed.

6

CARROT COCK AND A BUTTON NOSE

"What do ya mean they have to take another look?" A thick Jamaican accent rolled into my ears before my eyes fully opened. I'm alive and still in a bed. Around me, pale blue curtains drape from a metal bar. Even though mine aren't moving, it's clear that my neighbors are going in and out of their makeshift room.

"Ma'am, we are waiting on the surgeon to examine the sample," the audible conversation continued.

"We've been sitting here for hours, and my daughter hasn't been able to eat anything."

"I understand it's --" she is cut short.

"Madda!" A little girl starts to cry.

It could always be worse.

The lights were on as my senses adjusted to consciousness. I began picking up on details from all around. The steady beep of my heart rate monitor snatched my attention. Beeps were a real thing? I thought that only existed in television shows where people were about to die. Was I about to die? Shit. Am I already dead? In between the brief thoughts of a heart failure and the swelling frustrations of my neighbor, I looked down at another swell. A miniature mountain of bandage wrap hid what I could only hope was my genitalia. I needed to look. With a wiggle of my toes, I signaled to the rest of my body that it's time to move. My right arm, tethered to an IV, slowly moved to the burial site where Lucky used to be. Have I mentioned that the name of my penis is Lucky? Well, it was at least. I named it in high school in the most ironic of ways. Lucky if someone besides myself touches it, finds it, etc etc. I know, I'm hilarious. One of my best friends had a car he had also named Lucky. He drove an old, beat up Bronco with one speaker and doors that barely hung on. Even as a virgin, my dick humor was strong. That being said, I haven't called my dick Lucky for quite some time. The jury is out on whether it's more or less appropriate now.

My semi-stiff arm (as in, actual arm) braised over the blanket to see what kind of equipment might be underneath. I didn't feel much, but that's nothing new. One cloth had another bandage right under it. Under those bandages, a tube ran down my leg. Anyone who's been in surgery knows the odd feeling of being helpless. Even though I was awake for all of 45 seconds, I wanted to know what was happening. I mostly wanted to know if I still had a penis, but that secret was tightly wrapped beneath me. I had neither the strength nor the lack of intelligence to mess with anything.

"Good morning good morning." A friendly voice slipped through the curtains. The nurse had to be of Bermudian descent. The only reason I know that is because it's Bermudian culture to always greet people before asking questions or making statements. If you were to go up to a local in Bermuda and say "Excuse me, is this Front Street?" They would immediately know you're a tourist. If it's an elder, they're more likely to repeat 'good morning' until you repeat it back for the sheer sake of teaching respect.

"Good morning good morning," I instinctively respond.

"Looks like you had a nice sleep, how are you feeling?"

"Like a million bucks." What I really wanted to do was quote Ludacris lyrics and say "looking, smelling like a million bucks, ah!" but I didn't because then she might've sent me to a different part of the hospital. Obscure lyrical references probably aren't a thing in hospitals, or anywhere really. After the nurse essentially baby-birded me some water, the doctor popped in.

"Hi Ross, how are you feeling?" Dr. Casey had been in the night before to deliver the best case and worst case scenarios. Sitting down next to me, he smiled and opened a manila folder. Why hospitals still use paper files, I don't know. I do know, but still seems like a waste.

"I have some preliminary results from your surgery, which went very well." I take my first internal sigh of relief. "It seems the trauma was a bit greater than we anticipated." Dr. Casey's first language was not English, and this curtailed his capacity for small talk.

"Interesting," I inserted.

"Yes, well quite honestly Ross, you had the best possible outcome from pretty much the worst possible scenario." I believe that statement is the medical equivalent to a backhanded compliment. I quickly repeat it in my head in hopes to decode what he actually meant. I assumed this was a common practice in every patient's head when speaking to doctors.

You had the worst possible outcome from the best possible scenario. *Wait.*

You had the best possible outcome from the worst possible scenario. That sounded good.

"That's good, right?"

"Yes sir, very good indeed."

"So what exactly does that mean?"

Best possible case…

"The penis is made up of three parts," Dr. Casey began to explain. He leaned over to the vegetable plate next to me and picked up two carrots and a piece of celery.

"This is your urethra," he said highlighting the celery stick. "It's what you urinate through. These two parts on top are spongy tissues that fill up with blood during an erection. They are your corpus cavernosum. Most people, when they break the penis, tear one of these two spongy tissues or fracture their urethra. You tore both of your capillaries," signaling at the carrots, "and *severed* your urethra." Dr. Casey picked up the celery and snapped it in half.

"Wait, what?" The words escaped my mouth from both confusion and incredulity of the doctor's organic illustration. I winced at the thought of my vegetable garden. What the hell was wrong with me?

"It is an extremely rare case," he said, answering the next question in my head. "We believe you are the thirteenth person on file for this kind of trauma." I didn't want to know what happened to the fellas who weren't on file.

"Does that mean my penis will be written about in medical journals?" I joked, but also wasn't joking.

"No, I don't think so. And that isn't necessarily a good thing." He was right, I guess. The obvious question came next.

"How exactly, like, why was it so bad?" I asked. Advanced medical verbiage followed in the coming sexual explanation.

"That's a great question," he indulged. "Based on what you and your girlfriend told us and what we saw on the inside, the best guess is the firmness of your erection allowed for minimal elasticity. As her vagina became smaller during intercourse, you pulled out and, in your concurrent motion to penetrate, missed -- causing the snap."

Snap was not a word I thought I'd ever associate with my penis. The doctor drew a picture to further illustrate how a fifth grader would've doodled everything. He put his hand on my shoulder, smiled, and left. Before I knew it, I was in my own private recovery room. This corner office boasted two windows, a standard definition TV, available seating for two, and a reclining bed. Two bags inflated and deflated around my calves every couple of minutes for blood flow; a reminder to my body that I still had legs.

I sat there in silence for an hour. I'd guess 70% of our existence is silent, which sounds pretty depressing even for a made-up stat. Someone needs to invent a device that records inner dialogue. Bose? I won't even charge for IP on that one. It might have been the drugs, but I had an emotional one-way conversation with my penis, or, at least, what was left of it.

Hey dude. Hope you're okay. That's pretty fucked up what happened, right? I mean not to kick you while you're down and all, but you complicate everything man. If you weren't around, I wonder which I'd be more of, better or bitter. I'd probably be better because my decisions wouldn't revolve around you. That's probably why women make good leaders. They only have one brain to contend with. Man, I'm really sorry. We've been through so much together. Do you remember that time I was trimming and missed? Damn, we thought that was bloody.

———

"Good morning child, how are you feeling?" A Jamaican nurse had entered the room. She was short, a bit portly, and loaded with sass.

"Never been better," I replied.

"Oh God bless you." My guess was that she read the file and knew I could use a couple blessings. She shuffled through the various drawers in the room. "Here's the remote to the TV darling. This is your power on button," she continued in her off-the-boat accent (or, more logically, off-the-plane? Also, is off-the-boat derogatory?), "and this is the control for your bed. You can incline as you like, and I'm going to be right around the corner if you need anything else."

"Thank you so much. Seems pretty self explanatory."

"You'd be surprised dear. Can I get you anything to drink for now?" Her vocal cadence was pleasantly soothing, which must be a requirement for trauma nurses.

"I think I'm okay for now. Um, what's your name ma'am?"

"Certainly not ma'am," she laughed, "notta old lady quite yet." Why do women get offended when I say ma'am? I've always thought that it was a polite thing to say, and it's an ingrained part of my rhetoric. Yes sir, yes ma'am. I've considered going straight gangster and using the full madam, but haven't watched enough British television yet for that to feel authentic.

"My name is Lovelie." Lovelie checked my legs, still being robotically pumped, and gave them a couple of human squeezes. She checked different parts of my body, but actively avoided the elephant in the room. Then, Lovelie bent down and picked up a thick plastic bag filled with yellow water.

What in the fuck is this?

"Your bladder must be feeling really full right now."

What in the fuck -- wait.

"Um, yeah kind of."

The yellow water was urine. She was emptying a bag of urine... *my* bag of urine. My eyes traced a tube that went from the bag under the blankets and into what I presume was still my penis. Holy shit. I had a catheter in. I didn't really know what a catheter was. Were they supposed to be painful? Painkillers must have been flowing heavily through my system. Painkillers weren't really a thing in my family, so I always assumed my senses worked. This is probably a good time to mention my body's insane resilience to drugs. Blame it on my Christian upbringing, but the Lord gave me a body ready to combat the effects of virtually every drug I tried. That being said, my body was numb. Mini me was numb. Lovelie was amped.

"Oh child I don't care what you did, but you had the whole room running a lot up and down the halls this morning. Everyone fixin' to take a look, takin' care of you." We magically laughed out loud together.

"I always wanted to be popular," I said.

"I don't care child," she continued through her laughter, "I mean they called in the whole lot of 'em. You're going to be okay and that's what matters. Dr. Herm and Dr. Rajiv take good care of a healthy young man such as yourself." I had yet to meet a Dr. Rajiv. I wondered who he was and what that meant.

"Here's a meal for you when you get a little hungry. Chicken with a little rice and some green beans. Keep the plate on upside down or it'll get cold, okay?" I struggled to pay attention. "Now I've also got your pills here if you start to feel a little bit of that pain creep up on ya." She continued to talk as I checked in with my body, contemplating how pill addiction starts. My internal debated ended quickly.

"Now, if you take too many of these pills you might get constipated and you might not be able to go to the bathroom." If there's one good way to keep people from popping pills, it's to threaten them with constipation. Lovelie also did that thing where she used a term and subsequently defined it just in case. Constipation doesn't seem to be that medical, but I trust she's had people not know before.

I was constipated once when I was eight years old. I had never felt a pain so great. My aunt was visiting our apartment in Orlando as the five-day mark passed without passing a log. She walked in to find her nephew writhing on the floor in pain. On the toilet, off the toilet, on the toilet, off the toilet. This merry-go-round of discomfort can best be described as trying to push out a monster truck tire made of concrete. Sure, there was some movement, but simply pushing wasn't going to cut it. My mom, God bless her, didn't have the internet to rely on in those days for home remedies. Luckily, my aunt (her sister) was significantly older and had experience with her senior friends. There was only one solution, and it was every kid's least favorite drink. Prune juice. Fucking prune juice. So there I was, a tyke with his traffic jammed, staring down the barrel of a glass. This muddy brown and purple drink had been poured out of a can because back then there were less hippies commercializing drinks that tasted like ass but were "good for you." Sip by sip, I drank this unimaginable horror. After finally getting a bowel movement, I lay on my stomach for an hour praying I'd never have to drink that shit again.

Lovelie's cautionary offer of food left me conflicted. I would either be passing on food, which I love, or risking the pain. The chicken looked at me with an obvious answer. I took two bites and reflected over the dry breasts of chicken. The first bite confirmed I shouldn't have eaten it, and the second bite confirmed that I should've stopped after the first bite. I pressed the power button on the TV. Naturally, it didn't work. I looked around the empty room and laughed. Hospitals suck.

7

I THOUGHT YOU WERE DEAD

"**D**ude. What the fuck!?"

Smiling in disbelief, William came in the door with an entrance to rival any 90s' sitcom uncle. Will is my roommate. He's a lovable, well-kept Asian guy who went out 5 nights a week, but always showed up when you needed him. I forgot I had sent him an email. Without having to text or confirm my room, he showed up and found me. In a time when everything has to be over-communicated (and people still find distractions or excuses), he really made me feel cared for. 'Who would show up at the hospital' was a new measure for friendship.

Will brought the one thing I needed more than anything else: my phone charger. My poor phone had been sitting dead by my side. Cut off from the world, I, too, felt dead. In an instant, I started remembering the emails I had sent. That's how Will knew where to go, of course. Will and I have a deep sexual history together. That is to say, all roommates have a sexual history together. And *that* is to say, we both knew each other's sexual history pretty well. When selecting a roommate in New York, one must evaluate cleanliness, schedule, and if they smoke weed. Will and I were aligned on these things, but, most of all, we had a trust and respect for each other that allowed us to be honest with random questions.

What girl buzzed up at 3am?

Whose shoes are these?

Why is there a vibrator in the dishwasher? Just kidding, we didn't have dishwashers in Manhattan.

Will and I became roommates at a time when both of us had really shitty break ups happening. We were both moving from Seattle to New York, and we both were leaving girlfriends behind that we loved. In keeping the parallels, we both didn't want to do long distance and, shortly after moving, both had months where we felt like that was a huge mistake. In my case, I really did myself in. My ex and I officially split one month after she came to visit. For a couple of weeks, I indulged in New York's transactional dating scene. I was, by no means, a saint, but the void was obvious. I missed her so much and began to plot my comeback. In a true over-the-top move, I started a journal of all our memories. That's right, I scrapbooked, bitches.

My ex scrapbook (screxbook?) was the sweetest, most time-intensive gift I'd ever made. I tend to keep notes and mementos in relationships as breadcrumbs to remember the little things. In case there's a wedding, I want to be like BAM... I love you more than you thought! For two months, I recounted stories, put in pictures, scribbled down playlists, pasted postcards, the whole damn thing. We'd sporadically talk, but she was busy with her new temp job (which kept her in Seattle when I moved) and the distance grew over the holidays. We talked after New Years, and the temp job sounded like it was getting serious. Ipso facto, I got serious. I planned a surprise trip back to give her the book, confess my love, and swoon her into New York to live happily ever after.

"You have so much to give to this world, and New York is the place for you," I dramatically rehearsed in my head. I rearranged that thought about twenty different ways. How many imaginary conversations do we have with people we love? Two months later, I texted her as I landed in Seattle, asking if she had dinner plans.

She was at the gym, obviously caught off guard – my plan was working! She said she could only grab a drink, and my nervous system went into a frenzy. When I saw her from across the street, I knew this was my truth. When I hugged her, my heart beat out of its cage, but I knew something was off. As we sat there drinking our Moscow Mules on 1st Avenue and Vine Street, I cut the small talk.

"I feel so weird sitting here right now," I mumbled, "I hate not knowing what's going on in your life, if you've been seeing other people." I pause for her to dismiss that, but she doesn't. "Which is totally fine," I backpedaled on a floor that was rapidly sinking beneath me. "Wait, are you..."

She had already started seeing someone she knew from high school. Of course, she said she was going to tell me, but she hadn't found the right time. My body had physically reacted, swelling tides of shakes and apocalyptic thoughts. How could I be so dumb? Was this karma? The rest of that conversation was nothing but white, blank pages. I was too late. I was sunk.

Back in New York, Will tried to get me out for two months. I look back and laugh a bit at just how depressed and antisocial I was. I didn't eat, barely slept, and all the while I knew there was nothing to do to get her back. I left. There was a finite limit on the win-them-back scale, and I've been on both sides. With Will going through a break up, too, we spent a lot of nights talking about how crazy we both were being. Enough to get me out of my mind and to move forward. When I came out of it, New York took me right back in. It's so cliché, but things happen for a reason. She was this amazing woman who would happily live and die where she was born, and that wasn't the type of partner for me. I still have that screxbook, and I'm keeping it as proof that, if I'm lucky enough to have kids one day, it's possible to survive a devastating heartbreak.

———

"Nikki?" Will asked, looking to see if anyone was around. I nodded.

"Dude, you have no idea." Willy had a small, exasperated gasp that signaled the coming of a good story.

"So last night, I get home, *wasted*," he said, although this was not uncommon. "Your door is open, which I'm like, weird." He was always out later than me.

"I go in your room to get the Tylenol, and as I'm grabbing it off your headboard I see a shit ton of blood on the sheets. Which I'm like, oh you hooked up with a girl on her period. Gross, but, fuck, whatever -- we've both done worse. I pass out in my bed and wake up, bang, to someone knocking on my room door. What do I see? The silhouette of a girl just *sobbing*. I would say crying, but I've seen a lot of girls cry and this girl was SOBBING. Mind you, I'm barely awake.

Will? She asks. I freeze. I mean, I'm frozen. Dude, I'm frozen. The blood, you not there... it fucking clicks. You're dead. I thought you were dead. I honestly thought you were dead. I was like, oh fuck, this girl killed you and she's about to tell the story of how it happened. Some freak accident or something and now I've got to find a new roommate." To be fair, double rent would be tough to cover. He continues with the free entertainment.

"This girl is stressed. I ask her if she wants to get food, and she, actually I don't think she answered because all she could do was cry, but I get up, still drunk, and we go to that Moonlight Diner on Second." Will was one of those people who could hide his intoxication really well, not that Nikki would have noticed. Regardless, Willy's campaign for best friend ever continued.

"We're sitting by the window, sitting there listening to her and I don't know what to say. But I'm sitting there and everyone keeps looking at me like -- been there bro."

"So essentially," I interject to give him a breath.

"So essentially," he jumps right back in, "I went through a breakup for you without ever getting laid."

"Best Friend Ever," I award him.

"Best friend ever," he echoes right back. Good Guy Will, being kind to a stranger that he thought killed his roommate not but five minutes prior.

———

Pictures. That's what I thought of as my phone powered on. For whatever reason, I had the awareness to take a picture of the crime scene when this all started. Once I was moved to the OR, the hospital kept my phone so I didn't have anything after being admitted. As the welcome screen loaded, Will had a lot of questions, and he wasn't sure that he wanted the answers.

"Do I want to see it?" Will asked. He didn't. I wasn't sure I did either, but I went right to my photos for a look. The last picture on my camera roll was the one we'd been waiting for. It was bad. I stared at the picture in disbelief that the penis pictured was indeed mine. It looked like a broken nose that, while waiting to be reset, got hit with an oversized, cartoon hammer. Lucky's ringside crew hadn't stepped in to clean and blood still lingered on my leg. The flesh color hadn't changed into the purple it would become. Never in my life had I taken a dick pic before, and my first time sure was special. Honestly, I wish I had taken more dick pics so there could be a before and after comparison. I've just always found dick pics weird. Men naked look like weird aliens. Women naked look appealing with better design all around.

"Alright, let me see it," Will finally said after staring at my incredulous face. "Fuuucccccckkkkk!" he exclaimed with elongated letters. The longer we stared, the more details we noticed. Inflated like a balloon, neither of us could believe its contortion or its expansion.

"At least I got that nice trim," I noted of my freshly manscaped lawn. I wish that I had manscaped a week before so it looked more natural. Everyone likes that unkept/kept look, but I was on short notice. Before we could get much further, Dr. Wang entered.

"Hi Ross, good to see you again. How are you feeling?" Dr.

Wang asked. As I recall, she had wiggled a camera in my urethra for two minutes after calmly telling me I wouldn't need any more morphine. Small talk in the hospital was impossible, nonetheless we made some while she unwrapped my loincloth.

"You have a really nice room here with these windows."

"I agree. I'm assuming the manager sympathized with my cause."

"I'm Dr. Wang. I don't believe we met last night," she said to Will, introducing herself.

"I'm Will."

"Nice to meet you, Will. Don't feel too bad." Our heads both cocked to the side. Does she think we...

"Everything looks really good," she said, "Dr. Herm will be in shortly to let you know how surgery went."

Right after she nodded goodbye, she looked at Will and smiled. The door closed and we busted out laughing. Moving forward, we decided to establish that he did not perpetrate the crime. What's true and what's not true don't always matter, it's all about what people believe or want to believe. Three gentle knocks on the door precede Dr. Herm's entrance. The last time I saw this man, he majestically touched my shoulders and told me everything was going to be alright. This time, I hoped he would tell me everything was going to be alright while majestically touching something else.

Dr. Herm did just that, answering basic questions with patience and understanding. I had one question that wasn't as medical.

"What is my cover story?" I had been thinking about this question since I regained consciousness. In theory, I should've been sitting at work instead of laying in a hospital bed. The reasonable amount of time to go without contacting my boss was diminishing. Most excuses for a work absence were made up, and this would be no exception. I worked in Rockefeller Center, not Silicon Valley. After relaying that I wasn't comfortable with the honesty policy, Dr. Herm and I went through a couple options together.

- Option 1: Be honest. Tell my boss that I had a penile tear that requires little movement over the next two weeks, at which point my catheter will be removed and my mobility will be much better.
- Option 2: Illness. I've contracted a rare stomach flu that is affecting my nervous system, and that I will be able to work but shouldn't be around others because it is potentially contagious. The word contracted makes it sounds like an STD or a third world disease, each of which had their pros and cons.
- Option 3: Bike accident. In this freak scenario, I crashed my bicycle while I was riding in Manhattan and got impaled by a pole.

Why does the truth rarely present itself as a reasonable option? Probably because the truth sounds made up. So it was decided that from that moment on, I had been in an excruciatingly painful, freak bike accident. The word impaled had a certain ring to it that didn't invite questions. With a cover story and bandages for days, I wanted out of the hospital. The nurse wheeled me to the front and left me on the curb. In a wife beater, navy blue basketball shorts, Ray-Ban's, and a catheter visible to the world, I waited with Will for a Lyft.

8

GROUNDED

In third world countries, cattle have their heads tied to their leg so they don't run off. That's how I felt with my catheter in. Catheters are rubber tubes that connect a plastic bag, usually strapped to a person's leg, into their bladder via the urethra. The tube drains urine from the bladder into the bag, relieving the bladder muscle of its duty. Urine trickles down effortlessly with no need for the bladder muscles to do any work. It sounded like a nice rest, but a rubber tube tugged on my penis every time I moved. Catheters, also known as a Foley in the medical field, were mostly reserved for people over sixty.

Will opened the door to our Lyft, a Toyota Corolla, and we stared down our first real logistics problem. How do I get in the car without tugging this damn tube out? Tugs were unequivocally bad. One leg at a time, holding the handle on the inside roof of the car, I began my space mission into the backseat. Had this been a metered ride, my bank account would've cleared. Once the ride began, I dealt with the bumps. Every bump caused a tug, and, again, tugs are bad. For the twenty-minute ride home from the Upper East Side to the East Village, we drove over every damn pothole on 2nd Avenue. Now, look, I get it. Drivers don't sign up to be special assistants. But if someone is injured or has a newborn baby, they should probably change their normal gas-to-brake ratio. Otherwise passengers are prone to mutter passive aggressive phrases or ask to 'please take it easy.' Do I want to give a three-star rating for lack of passenger awareness? No. Will I? Probably not. I understand the collateral damage of social reviews, and my temporary disdain for someone shouldn't outweigh their need to provide for a family. But will I think about leaving a bad review? Ya damn straight, sucka.

As Will and I arrived to the corner of E 6th and 1st, we looked at the tower of stairs leading up to our apartment. My catheter and I stared at each other like a Mexican standoff. After a couple deep breaths, I channeled my inner Jordin Sparks and took it one step at a time. Slowly but surely, I made it back to the the scene of the crime, Unit 4D.

"I changed your sheets." Good Guy Will took my bloody sheets to the laundromat and endured the judgement that came with it.

"Thank you dude. Seriously. I'm well aware of how gross this is." The bed looked at me with disdain. We knew our time together was about to exponentially multiply. It was time for business. I needed to tie up the loose ends and get to work on everything I couldn't do for the next two weeks. First up, I had a trip to Vegas for a bachelor party and I needed to cancel my flight. I was a bit relieved to not be another guy going to Vegas with a group of guys. My theory regarding being a guy in Vegas was simple. There were four conditions in which you could have a good time.

1) You go on someone else's dime. This can be with a company, on a job, in someone's hype crew, or with your friend's friend who spends so much money playing poker that everything is comped.

2) You are a girl. This means you usually get in places for free on your own. If not, there are men of varying creep levels, both foreign and domestic, that want women in their company and will pay whatever cover or table minimums exist.

3) You are prepared to spend a lot of money. You are not a girl,

and no one in your crew has the hookup. You want to have fun, and you know that means you can't stay at the Golden Nugget.

4) You spend a lot of time at the $3 craps tables. You're always dressed up and ready to say yes in case you make wild friends that take you on a random adventure, pit stopping at a strip club at 3:30am because your taxi driver offers to take you there for free when you're just trying to go home.

I have done the first and last option. This upcoming trip would have been option three, and I hate a cover charge of any denomination. With all this philosophy behind me, I called Orbitz, the service I used to book the trip.

Hello and thank you for calling the Orbitz personal assistance line. If you are calling to make a new reservation, we encourage you to use our website. All bookings made over the phone will incur a $12 processing charge. Please refer to our website, orbitz.com, for online bookings. If you are calling about current reservations, or to cancel, please say so now.

Automated customer service blows my mind on many levels. First, there should be no charge to do this over the phone. If anything, we should get credit for having human interaction and salvaging jobs. Some customer service agents are as helpful as talking to a dial tone, but at least there's hope. Second, if I am calling and your business is strictly based on a website, you don't need to tell me to go to your website. This is the equivalent to having IT tell someone to restart their computer. Sometimes I forget that too, but that doesn't make it okay. Third and final point, I absolutely do not like voice commands on the phone. I feel like an idiot; the people around me judge me; the damn computer makes alien noises when it decodes what I'm saying; and it always makes me repeat myself.

I'm sorry, I couldn't understand you. Try using words like "help" or "change reservation." I dialed 0 to expedite the process.

"Thank you for calling the Orbitz helpline, this is Deborah, how can I be of assistance to you today?" I imagined Deb to be a kind woman. She had a full-bodied, yet soft voice that I was not expecting. I try and repeat the agent's name to acknowledge their existence, but they usually mumble. This was so I couldn't report them later since odds were they would not be able to help. Unfortunately, Deb's diction was exceptional.

"Hi Deborah," I say to establish a kinship where helping me would be the right thing to do, "I need to cancel a flight due to an accident I was in yesterday."

"I'm so sorry to hear that, I can help you choose the best option." Deborah asks me to send over documents from my doctor, which I do, and then proceeds with a few more questions.

"Thank you for your patience sir. Before we proceed, I need to ask you a few questions for security purposes, is that ok?"

"Of course."

"Thank you. Can I have your date of birth please?

"Are you at the same address?

"Is this your primary phone number?

"When you registered with Orbitz, you provided a security answer. Can you please tell me the first name of your first pet?"

My last pet was a dog. Before the beloved family dog, I had a lot of pets that could qualify as the first, but they didn't last very long. They either died (bag of goldfish), escaped (Snickers and Snowflake the hamsters), or were returned (Mickey the parakeet). In the plethora of security answers I could have possibly given, not one came to mind as the absolute correct one.

"I'm sorry, I can't remember that particular one. Too many botched pets growing up."

She didn't laugh. "All right, sir, not a problem." It was a problem, but sure. "You can also go online to process this request." I don't think she was aware that her suggestion eliminated the need for her current job. For her sake, I decline.

"Not a problem..."

———

The next item on the agenda was the all-inviting call to my parents; the sympathy-seeking, but-not-in-an-obvious-way, telephone conversation to inform them that their prodigal son had been involved in a systematically God-forsaken, yet undeniably unfortunate accident. It's one of those things you dread doing but have to do in textbook fashion. God knows I would need some support over the next few weeks.

"Hello. Are you watching the news?" My mom answered. She was always watching the news.

"No I'm not," I replied, bracing myself for the ensuing conversation. After an update on terrorist activities around the world, my mom asked how I was doing. With a calming tone, I began my symphony.

"Everything's okay, but I had to spend the night in the hospital."

"Oh God, are you okay?" The comedy of asking if someone's okay after leading with everything being okay was natural.

"Yes, I'm fine. Long story short, I was having sex with a girl last night and broke my penis. Had to go to the emergency room and have surgery, and now I'm here."

A beat, and then two. That awkward pressing silence. Not a sigh to be heard, or the rustle of leaves. I could even do with a chirping cicada right about then, but nothing. I really did not expect what happened next, although I should have. After all, this was the person whose womb I twiddled my thumbs in while awaiting deliverance. She rolled out a calm and collected statement.

"Okay, well, I'm going to book my flight right now. Please don't be stupid, I still want grandchildren."

I did not follow the rest of what my mom said, mostly because I was much too preoccupied with the mental and physical preparation necessary in the coming weeks. Despite the impending life lessons that my mom would be delivering, I needed someone to help me out. Moms were always going to be there no matter what. No questions asked, at least at first. That being said, moms were going to find anything possible to worry about. Hakuna Matata didn't compute...

The pillow's too high; my belt's too tight; the mole on the back of my neck might be cancerous. I've got a little jello in my eye that could be jaundice; I shouldn't drink; I shouldn't drive; what kind of detergent am I using to wash my sheets? For over a decade, my mom's sole responsibility on Earth was to take care of me. That has become harder to do as time has gone on, but I knew there was no one more willing to be there for me. For everyone's sanity, my brother James said he'd come as a buffer.

Once all the phone calls were taken care of, I settled back into home base. My domain beckoned; the crisp full bed upon which I would lay throughout recovery. Growing up, I slept in a lot of beds: from ones with groaning springs, to others with creaking headboards and high polished oak legs, to the futon that magically served as both couch and bed. Through all of that, I never once felt that I had been sleeping on a doctor's table, until then. Surrounded by an assortment of wipes, gauze, and Q-tips, I lay. I was prepared for surgery every hour of every day. My survivor's guide to being bedridden included a rarely written-in diary, a copy of The Last Lecture, an XBOX, and a tray to put my sippy cup on. With my bed set up, I needed to get the one thing that mattered. Painkillers.

9

RX BANDITS

W ill informed me that the pharmacy down the street closed at six o'clock, which was in twenty minutes. Nothing in New York closes that early in the evening. Breakfast places don't even close that early. I stuck my feet in some sandals and headed out. The otherwise quick trip turned into an epic slog, each shuffling step competing with the next. The entire neighborhood stared at my sweatpants fashion as they took the passing lane around me, many looking back as they continued forward. I glanced at my wristwatch. Ten minutes to six. With the catheter as my ball and chain, it had taken me ten minutes to get outside and go a mere two blocks to the store. The pharmacy was, of course, at the back. Shuffling through the double automatic doors, I could see the finish line, which also had a line. One woman was being served at the counter and an elder woman stood behind her in line. She turned around, gave me a quick scan head to toe and pulled the corners of her mouth down.

"Rough day?" She asked in her local accent, split between over-caring Jewish mother and longtime New York resident. I puffed a smile out because only in New York would I get genuine sympathy via geriatric sarcasm.

"It could be worse." The smile became a smirk across my face, and I couldn't help but chuckle. Being as laughter was contagious, she let out a little too.

"Well, they better not close up now that I've made it this far," she said.

The young man behind the counter cleared his throat and announced, "Um last customer, ma'am, last customer."

The repeat of the last line was delivered directly to me. Sometimes, it was those little things that made me tick, and a little Denzel Washington voice pops into my head. This white-coat mother fucker had some kind of nerve to look me right in the eye. I cocked my head to the side as though to say 'my man' and show him a gun at my hip. At the same time of this imaginary hood moment, I felt my stomach sink to the floor. Why is this shit always happening to me? The tube in between my legs giving an extra uncomfortable twitch as though to affirm the series of misfortunes.

"Excuse me sir. I've just come out of surgery, is it possible to-"

"I'm sorry, we have to close at 6. We'll be open tomorrow morning at 7."

I looked at him the way a girl looks at her boyfriend when he's forgotten their anniversary. A mixture of frustration, disappointment, anger, sadness, and acceptance clouded my face as I contemplated what to do.

"This young man can take my place then," grandma said, signalling towards me. I think the pain was reflected in my eyes.

"Oh that's okay ma'am, although very kind of you," I said as the natural human reaction to resist kindness escaped.

"I'll tell you what," she said, turning back to the dickhead behind the counter, "I'll have my go if you agree to see this young man too."

"Ma'am, it's store policy and -"

"I mean it, if you don't see him too, you don't get to see me and I'll be ringing in with some serious complaints about you, young man." He may have been an emotionless, overworked grad, but he wasn't going to test the will of a stand-in Jewish mother. He paused and then agreed. My fairy godmother took all of two minutes before finishing.

"You are most welcome, and what a rude young man trying to put a hard stop on someone that's just come out of surgery. You take care of yourself then." She looked right at the guy behind the counter when she said, "What a rude young man." Old people don't give a shit. They've earned that.

"Thank you, I really appreciate you doing this," I said to the jackass behind the counter. Even if the food's cold, be nice to the waiter.

As my guardian angel shuffled out of the pharmacy, a solution to my immobility presented itself. Lying in the clearance bin, two canes awaited my purchase. A cane would serve as both support and an indicator to everyone around me to proceed with caution. Two canes lay there, each designed for a different personality. One cane had a tropical pattern all over it and the other was plain brown. I was born in Miami, so the choice had already been made.

Back at home, I laid out my medications and picked up the Cialis first. Cialis is the updated version of Viagra. Viagra is a pop-and-play drug. Once it goes down the hatch, the erection goes up and famously lasts for up to four hours. God bless. With Cialis, a man can get erect on his own time. Cialis puts boner fuel in the tank so that someone doesn't have to be waiting in the wings for immediate foreplay. As I understand it, both drugs increase blood flow to a man's johnson. The goodie bag of drugs also contained some painkillers. One quick Google search was all it took to confirm that the Oxycodone in my hand was the shit everyone gets hooked on.

My first real experience with painkillers came at the dentist office. Despite my best efforts to put it off, I had to get my wisdom teeth removed when I was 17. The dentist offers two options for patients undergoing this operation: local or general anesthesia. Going back to my catastrophic insurance plan, the choice was obvious. General anesthesia would be more expensive, so I took nine shots of Novocain to the gums instead.

"If you start to feel any sort of pain or feeling, just squeeze on my arm," the dentist said. I immediately went to the worst case scenario. Why wouldn't nine shots be enough? Isn't this what you do? Then I began to wonder if they charged per shot. Was this a scam? High possibility they were trying to sucker me, and I didn't like getting suckered even as a teenager. Nine is an awfully odd number. I have four corners in my mouth, and nine isn't divisible by four. Eight should have done the trick, unless the standard is twelve... ZING! Pain interrupted my basic math and shot through me. Pain from a tooth was a special brand of pain. I spread out my fingers and gripped the chair, trying not to be a little bitch or an interruption to the man pulling teeth from my mouth.

"Arh. Alggh," I said to the dentist from the back of my throat.

"Are you feeling anything?" If I was asked this in my adult life, probably not. But as a soft, pubescent seventeen year old, I felt it all.

"Okay, Charlotte let's give him a little more numbing." This was one of those moments with a doctor where I yell WHAT THE FUCK in my head. I didn't curse out loud that much as a kid because Jesus was always listening, but, in my head, such boundaries didn't exist. Anxiety occupied the rest of my time with that dentist as I wondered if the painkillers would finish faster than the surgery.

Back at my apartment, I carefully read the instructions prescribed on the side of the cannister. I placed each pill on my tongue and scooted it towards the back of my mouth before sipping a little orange juice. I have always preferred to take pills with OJ because taking pills always sucked and OJ was always delicious. Being that I was a husky kid, I also liked that medication provided another excuse to eat. With the meds setting in soon, there was one more job to do. I lifted up my medical mumu, looked at the bandages beneath, and channeled *The Lion King*.

"It is time," I said with my best Rafiki impression. It was time to take off the medical wrap and examine the full monty post surgery.

Its current look wasn't great. The head of my sad penis poked out of its cotton wrapping like a hobo in the winter. The discolored skin looked as though it came straight out of a domestic violence case. Shades of purple, blue, and pink mixed around like a Bob Ross palette after ten seasons. The catheter tube going into my penis hole (not sure the technical term) appeared to be an oversized straw freshly poked into a fountain soda. It was simultaneously gross and hilarious. I blankly stared at it the way a student looked at a piece of modern art. I hadn't had the urge to examine my Dong Juan since the hospital, and this first look validated that instinct.

I began to unravel the little toy soldier from his blankets. I would've put off staring at the beast, but I needed to clean it with Bacitracin. Bacitracin, an antibiotic ointment, prevented infections and any further inflammation in the battle zone. As the wrap came off, the true "holy shit" moment revealed itself. A circumference of stitches, eighteen in total, popped in and out of my doughy dragon. The dark stitch line felt like a rugged lasso squeezing my two halves together. I still found it mind boggling that the incision was circular, like Frankenstein, instead of filleting my little guy up and down. There was something *Silence-of -the-Lambs*-esque about the fact that they pulled the skin up and down in order to operate that irked me.

What had become of my beloved? The cotton jockstrap pinned little Hamlet up as I prepared the Q-tips with Bacitracin. I swabbed on my cob with gentle dabs to minimize the stinging. I'll admit that this caretaking felt oddly therapeutic. There wasn't much pain either until about half way through, when I managed to catch a cotton swab on one of the stitches.

"Eeeeee!" I sounded out on the inhale of a breath. I was being over dramatic, but it felt like one wrong move would unwind the situation and thus my man parts. Luckily, I finished the job without another reason to visit the ER. As I threw away various medical supplies, the drugs politely kicked in. It wouldn't be long before my reinforcements arrived.

10

THE MOTHERSHIP

In one corner stood my mother, commonly referred to as Mommy. That always has been and always will be her name. Having said that, I understand the social concerns when I, in my twenties, try and get her attention by yelling "Mommy!" in public.

A beautiful woman in her mid-sixties with dark blonde hair, my mom believed she was a medical professional. This was mostly due to the advent of sites like WebMD and trendy blog articles. My mom legitimately had too much love to give, and she would do anything to help someone in need. I was mentally prepared to be that person. Her arrival always came equipped with an abundance of internet advice on what to eat, when to sleep, and how celebrities were discovered (aka career advice). James, my older brother, arrived soon after. He was the archetype of a first born and a friendly neighborhood do-gooder. After two internships in college, he took a job in Seattle with Microsoft. He was the first to leave the comforts of Florida, setting the precedent for me to do the same. We weren't close growing up, and the first real conversation we had was after he went through a big college break up. He was the computer robot trying to handle heartbreak and I was the artist shepherding him through emotions. After that, our relationship only grew. We are almost five years apart, but we have extremely odd parallels. When he was my exact age, he also went through some medical trials. Unlike mine, his issues weren't because of nefarious activities. James was diagnosed with multiple sclerosis, or MS, an autoimmune disease with no known cause or cure that varied in its degenerative effects. Remember when I said there's a difference between someone asking "how are you doing" versus "how are you feeling?" I learned that from him. My friends stopped asking how he was and began asking how he was feeling.

Now, it's unfair to introduce someone by leading with their health condition, but it's hard to gauge the strength of his character without knowing. Living with or beating a disease required incredible emotional resilience and his selfless approach to this medical revelation readjusted my appreciation for life. After he was diagnosed, I moved from New York to Seattle permanently. Sitting through doctor appointments, I had trouble comprehending what was happening inside of my brother's body. He looked completely normal. Even though I moved out there to be by him, I didn't have a job and it was the worst time to be looking. I lived on his couch for a year while working every production job I could find, and I can't definitively say who was taking care of whom. Point being, we've gone back and forth being there for one another and it was my turn to call one in. As kids, he looked like Egon from Ghostbusters. Now that he doesn't have hair, he looks like a thinner version of Steve Ballmer. Consistent nerd levels existed through his whole life.

"Where are your paper towels?" Moms are always cleaning, and mine wasted no time in relaying her thoughts on dust. "I don't even know how you breathe in here. I wish you would clean so you can breathe. I'm not asking much. How do you concentrate?" Not too sure how concentration and dust correlate, but logic generally doesn't apply when dealing with her. Usually, I would avoid this berating by a deep clean before she arrived, but I was a bit restricted. I considered hiring a cleaning lady, but even then, a certain amount of pre-clean is necessary. I get anxiety if I don't pre-clean before the main clean when hiring a cleaner. The lack of logic might be genetic.

"Did you wash your hands today?" My mom also lived for hand sanitizer. This ask was only stage one of her momming, of which there were three.

Stage one.

- Email articles. Ones that didn't require a reply. In my mom's case, they were usually from the staple mom websites (Good Morning America, TODAY, CBS, or whatever network Anderson Cooper is on. She loves him. All women love him).
- Diet advice. What to eat, when to eat, and generally to make sure that I'm eating at all.
- Updates on her friends' daughters' relationship statuses. The ultimate win for a parent must be matchmaking. That would ensure she "came from a good family."
- When to get a haircut.

Stage two.

- Emails where the subject line is a question. The question is in all caps and has multiple question marks at the end. ARE YOU WATCHING 60 MINUTES??? Then, a follow up call asking why she hasn't heard back.

Mom: Did you get my email?
Me: Yes, I wrote you back.
Mom: Oh that's your response?

- Fashion commentary. This was a double-edged sword. On one hand, my mom would tell me I'm the most beautiful person in the world every time she'd look at me. As a result of this, she wanted to contribute to my apparel like it was 20 years ago. As a result of that, my mom would spend all her excess time shopping for me in every discount clothing store around (Marshall's, Ross, TJ Maxx, Nordstrom Rack). A mom doesn't walk out of a store empty handed. My mom would buy clothes, send pictures of them to me, get upset when I didn't want them, and then return everything.

"Oh, you're too good for Marshall's now?"

- Facebook stalking potential girlfriends. My mom would send names of the aforementioned friends' daughters and then ask for my opinion. Do I think they're pretty? If not, I should meet them anyway.

"Don't be so stubborn. You never know."

- Insistence that shaving would be nice.

Stage three.

- Email about her friend's daughter (probably a dental hygienist) maybe moving to New York and how it'd be nice if we would meet up to "make your mother happy" with a picture attached of a large, black Eddie Bauer jacket that she was "lucky to get," if I wanted it. CC'd on this email would be both her friend and her friend's daughter.
- Follow up email about a haircut that she offered to pay for.

I once made an offhand comment to one of my friends about the number of links my mom sent to me, he replied, "...at least you still have a mom." I've since shut the fuck up on that one. Moms guilty of momming want the best. They weren't always sure how to go about it or what's in their power to change. All she knew was that she was there to take care of her baby, and caretaking an injured cub was what moms do best.

"We'll need to pick up some dish soap and cotton wool. Do you have an ice pack? Don't sit up, I'll get it. Did you wash your hands since you were on the phone? That phone is filthy. I'm going to go get some fruit." Her stream of consciousness became a sort of guided meditation over time.

"Mommy." James didn't need to say anymore. Simply stating someone's name in my family was a common method of getting them to pause. We all took turns playing this role depending on who was dishing out the advice. In this case, my mom was busy momming and that meant James came in to softly tap the brakes.

"Is there a Costco anywhere close?" My mom knew what she liked and stuck to what she knew, and she knew Costco. She wanted a deal wherever she went, but who doesn't? There was one Costco in Manhattan on the Upper East Side, and it was a pilgrimage to get there. Much like IKEA, it's a place most New Yorkers only visit once every three years. Since storage wasn't really a thing, buying a 48-pack of toilet paper or four gallons of milk made little sense. Yet, my mom persisted.

"Mommy, there are half a dozen bodegas within a five-block radius." A bodega is a small convenience store in NYC, usually on a street corner. They always magically have whatever you need at all times.

"Ok, first thing's first then, I need to head to the drug store," started my mom.

"I've already picked up my prescriptions."

With authority, my mom looked at James and declared, "AJAX," which was her preferred brand of toilet cleaner.

"Of course," my brother replied, choosing his battles wisely. My mom and James got ready to leave as I popped another pill. The Oxycodone numbed my nerve endings. I remembered that one of my favorite artists was painting a mural on a wall about six blocks north. For about two years, I had been running a street-art Instagram account that amassed over 10,000 followers. That's enough to get excited about, but not nearly enough to get laid for. The artist, a guy who went by Jerkface, had started painting a Charlie Brown mural on the side of a brick building that overlooked a playground. It was slated to be the largest mural in downtown Manhattan.

"Where are you off to?" my mom asked, noticing the shoes were back on my feet and keys were jangling in James's pocket.

"Gonna go check out some street art," I said.

"Do you want me to come?" she asked.

"I'm going to go with him. Brother time," James said as the buffer.

"I'll be fine Mommy, thank you."

"Okay," she paused, awaiting her next thought. "When was the last time you washed your sheets?" She was truly adorable.

We covered six blocks in forty-five minutes, allowing James and me to shoot the shit and laugh a little. Tragedy and trauma bring people together, and we did just that. I filled him in on Parker. I needed to talk about it more than he needed to hear it.

"I emailed you, Will, and her. The last thing I wanted to do was be all fucked up after surgery and try and give a coherent explanation."

He knew I had to call her, and this would be one of few chances for privacy. Sometimes the streets of New York were the most private places to be. As Audrey Hepburn said, "New York is the only place I can go to be alone." Okay, I actually don't know if she said that, but it sounds like something she would've said (I think). James resumed normal human pace, and soon, I was alone. I had five blocks and thirty more minutes until home. It was time to call Parker.

11

BREADSTICKS

S ome say love doesn't come easy. People in successful relationships say if it doesn't start easy then it's probably not right. My relationship with Parker couldn't have had a tougher trial to start. But let's back up a bit. Who was Parker? The blue-eyed, blonde-haired one-of-a-kind wonder woman who, within no time at all, became the apple of my eye.

We met at an adult summer camp. I'll repeat that. Adult summer camp. My friend started a business where he rented out kids' camps for a weekend, filled them with 100 adults, and added alcohol. Somewhere in the mountains of upstate New York, we played, danced, and drank for three days. No cell service meant no cell phones dragged us into the digital world. Like being on a cruise, the single people at camp had a finite amount of time to survey the field and choose who to pursue. I remembered Parker from the bus ride up. I'm a sucker for blue eyes and blonde hair, both of which she had on stellar levels. Only one of the five girls I've dated in my life had blue eyes and blonde hair (she had some blue hair too), but I would still shuffle those traits under 'my type.'

By the second day, we had encountered each other maybe three times. Then it happened. Our first physical contact. We were playing ultimate frisbee on opposite teams, and I guarded her tighter than OJ's glove.

"Y'all wanted equal rights!" I barked in her face, guarding her from throwing the frisbee. Parker's competitive nature came out and she playfully pushed me over. My theater degree came into play as I flopped and called for a foul. She kicked my shoe as she shuffled back into the game. I wish I could say that the first time was more intimate, and it wasn't until the dance party that night that I saw her again.

I have an extremely ineffective tactic of talking to women that I think are cute. When out at a bar or a party, I'll do about three flybys in a girl's line of sight to see if we catch eyes. If we do, I usually immediately look the other way and blow it. Sometimes, if our smiles meet, I once again turn away as though I wasn't doing exactly what I was doing. In the *rarest* of cases, I'd do a flyby, smile, and then say hi. Saying hi started the road to either redemption or rejection. Saying hi should be easier for me, but I am pretty bad when it comes to breaking the ice. In the case of my flybys with Parker, no looks were exchanged. I made my third pass only to see her making out with another guy. Like a goldfish with a short term memory, I moved right back to the dance floor and made out with another girl. To get it, you've got to be willing to let it go.

———

"Your pockets aren't properly stitched." Parker spoke to me, half asleep, in her posh accent as I stood in the aisle on the bus ride back to the city. The rules of engagement are subtle and almost too easy to overdo. Truthfully, Parker saying anything in my direction surprised me after camp ended. We bantered back and forth in a post-party-weekend haze about cultural differences between the US and the UK. She hadn't been in the states for long and we exchanged a lot of "You haven't been to ___?!" The more I learned, the more I liked. Her energy and curiosity made me giddy. I'd love to say that we cuddled up next to each other soon after we started talking. But we didn't. I retreated back to the seat next to where my camp make-out girl sat. She promptly fell asleep on my shoulder while I hoped Parker wouldn't walk by and see. You know that feeling of going into a grocery store and then leaving without buying anything? Yeah, that's the undeserving guilt I had at the moment. Being with someone and thinking about someone else wasn't a crime, but the last thing I wanted to do was knock off the idea of there being a chance.

———

For our first date, I mapped out a line of American staples for her to experience, starting with dinner. A quick succession of texts primed the stunt I had in store.

Me: They don't take reservations, but I put our name in. I'll be downstairs in 10.

Her: Ok ok ok… serious with formal?

Me: Not full formal, just nice.

Her: Dress?

Me: Only to start.

Her: Ross…

Me: Gottem

Her: Heels?

Me: Heel yeah

Her: Oy.

My best friend Diego and I were fat kids growing up, and some of our detailed eating traditions were proof. We existed to eat, play, and do theatre. The biggest treat as a kid was going out to eat at one of Orlando's acclaimed chain restaurants. Each place carried an association. Some examples…

Dairy Queen: At the end of Little League season, the team could order anything. I'd get the Butterfinger Blizzard, no debate.

TGI Friday's: The wrap of a play meant everyone involved

earned a meal in the land of potato skins and Jack Daniel's flavored sauces.

Sweet Tomatoes: Someone died. This upscale buffet (if such a place exists) accommodates a lot of people and had focaccia bread, which was fancy foreign food before that was a thing.

Diego and I had a birthday food tradition that stood the test of time, and it's no coincidence that this special Italian restaurant centered around family. The Olive Garden became a pillar of our brotherhood that, no matter what the year had brought, offered a chance for us to reset our values, goals, and carbs. Diego always stuck to the Tour of Italy. I never waned from the chicken fettuccini alfredo, allowing the sauce to pull double duty on the endless breadsticks. Even though it wasn't my birthday, I wanted to take Parker to a place that was a part of my history. She made the mistake of telling me she'd never been. Strictly for comedic purposes, I wanted us to be in formal attire at this incredibly cheesy restaurant.

"It's buzzing!" I said. I held the red brick vibrator, a historic piece of technology that restaurants use to notify patrons about availability. The pace picked up. Parker, in her casual black dress and small heels, looked incredibly pretty. I almost felt bad she spent so much time getting dressed up for the night I had planned, but I was too excited for my reveal to think about it. The OG, as the homies call it, was mentioned in our first conversation. Comedians refer to this as a callback.

"You can't be serious."

"I can't be more serious," I opened the double glass door and gestured my hand inward. She realized she'd been duped as I coerced her into a smile. "My lady."

In an instant we had been transported into a poor man's version of a poor man's version of Tuscany. The overflowing AC froze our nostrils to mask the years of garlic and cream sauce that had settled into the faded carpet. I took Parker's soft, white hand by the fingertips and looked at her with the biggest smile on my face. I truly entertained myself.

"This is really quite special." She couldn't help but laugh as we passed screaming children and oversized adults to our table. "Fantastic suggestion to wear heels." We looked at each other across our two-top table covered in picture menus and smiled. Even though we came from different economic upbringings, she embraced my roots.

The idea of marrying rich has been pervasive throughout my (and probably everyone's) life. I knew that wouldn't work for me early on when my parents, God bless them, were offered a sort-of dowry by a family friend. About twice a year, our family would visit another Armenian family, the Hagosians, at their mansion (according to the Florida definition of "mansion"). The scene was the same every time. The women cooked, talked about their kids, and drank wine in the kitchen area. The men sat on the patio drinking bottled beer, smoking cigars, and essentially having a poetry slam with each other in Armenian. My dad, who spoke three languages, ripped a mean rhyme. He didn't get to use his native tongue often and, even though he didn't smoke or drink more than one beer, it was fun to watch him unwind. In the old country, the men would sit in circles and rhyme about each other in rounds. There was no beat or hype crew, just the cleverness of their wit with the Armenian language. Even though I don't speak Armenian or Arabic, I like to think my dad's foreign poeticism gave me a genetic pre-disposition to being a rapper. Like a true artist, my dad was the only one in that group who wasn't a doctor. He immigrated to the US for school, and took only math classes his first two semesters while he learned English. He moved here with practically nothing and lost the little he did have when his Boston apartment got robbed. Parents don't want their kids' lives to be shittier than theirs, and money was usually a big player in that equation. Sure, money doesn't buy happiness, but it does make life a lot easier.

Dr. Hagosian, the wealthiest of the group, had four daughters. Two of those were coincidentally the same ages as James and me. After two years of going to their house for various holidays, the setup collusion began. James had started college and was safely out of the running, but the younger daughter Yeraz was primed for a prince. I was 17 and more of a man than I'd ever been. The scarce chest hair must have been a sign for Dr. Hagosian to take me aside and ask about my future plans. I didn't think much of it until the car ride home when my parents made their case for Yeraz, which means "dream" in Armenian.

"You know she is a very pretty girl," my mom started, "and they have a very nice family." I'm the first to admit that attraction is highly subjective, but I was not attracted to Yeraz. She was the product of her traditional upbringing. She wore a lot of makeup, perfume, and colored contacts. Some people like that, but I don't. She also wasn't involved in any extracurricular activities. In grade school, no after-school activities was the equivalent to being willingly unemployed. That's not hot! But this wasn't entirely her fault. She'd been pampered by her father and modeled after her mother, who grew up in a vastly different culture. As a sapiosexual who enjoyed a more natural look, I did not see myself with her as even a stretch of a notion. I thought my parents were joking when they presented their case. They weren't joking.

"Dr. Hagosian really likes you, so maybe you shouldn't be so quick to rule her out. They are a very nice Armenian family and you would be taken care of." That last part had an echo to it. That last part led into the truth. Dr. Hagosian had informally offered my parents real estate for our future family plus one million dollars if we were to wed. *One million dollars!* Cue the Dr. Evil pinky. That was an inconceivable amount of money based on my Florida definition of rich. Like a truly naive soldier of love, I dismissed them and the Prince of Persia-like offer to spend eternity with this woman. As a hustler in training, the only thing I considered was how I could create a workaround to still get paid. Would my dowry vest after two years? Do dowries vest? Is this actually called a dowry? Also, what is vesting? Either way, I believed that all the comforts of money wouldn't make me happy. I was more of a hipster artist as an angry teenager than even I knew.

———

The affection between Parker and I multiplied over the next three months. With plenty of restaurants and events to go to in New York, we shared the quality and quantity of experiences in a few months that couples could only hope for in five years. I worked near where she lived, and convenience weighed heavier in my relationships than I'd like to admit. It wasn't what we were doing that attracted me to her, it was the parts of her that came out in our adventures that pulled me in. One of my litmus tests was to watch someone interact with a waiter. Anyone who's rude to their waiter gets an automatic X from me. I can confidently say that this is true for anyone who has ever worked in hospitality. One night, Parker and I went for an Italian dinner (not at the OG, unfortunately) and the foreign waiter struggled to answer our questions in English. After he left, she melted with sympathy for him.

"What a nice fellow! Ugh he was trying so hard to help us," she let out of her sad puppy face, "I just want to speak his language." Where some people would complain that this was America and they should speak English, Parker understood how hard it was to come to this country and make it. She treated the janitor like the CEO, and it attracted me to her on a visceral level.

Her company took up most of her time, and it had to. I helped everywhere I could and sometimes she even paid me for it. Start-up life was not glamorous and the people who own the business were often alone in their quest. In the beginning, I had no clue what that perspective looked like. There were times that I'd make fun of her canned speech to different media outlets that I shouldn't have, but we were growing together. This was the first time I'd ever been with someone who would rather stay home and create than go out and waste the night away. The balance between social life and work life merged together. I was being exposed to a world of driven people and unforgiving passion that I'd been shielded from in the corporate world. There was no eat, pray, love with us. For us, it was eat, work, play. And play was sex.

If it's not clear by now, I liked Parker a lot. Three months later, we sat in the thick of what was often referred as the "gray area" in the dating world. Common to the population of singles in New York, the gray area means two people see each other consistently without a verbal commitment. There was an understanding of togetherness without having a talk about it. This talk was commonly referred to as The Talk. The Talk was a conversation where the two in question tell each other that they like one another enough to stop seeing, sleeping with, or sexting others. Commitment in New York was, simply stated, an agreement to not snoop around with other people. It's safe to say that men usually prolong The Talk to do one more dumb thing. The idea that you can get dumb things out of your system was a fallacy. There will always be one more. I truly felt ready to flush everyone that wasn't her and, in a move often reserved for the female gender, decided to instigate The Talk myself. I thought about her incessantly, and my heart pined in a corner of uncertainty.

"Okay so, what are we doing?" I asked, pacing around her room as she packed for another business trip. With that one nondescript question, I launched us into a three-hour conversation. In grade school, that galvanizing, nondescript question sounded more like "Hey, what are you thinking about right now?" The initial answer to both of those questions never changed.

"I don't know."

For the first time in a long time, I had fallen for someone. That vulnerability had been vacant from my emotional circle for the past year and a half. After the heartbreak out of Seattle, I hadn't thought of anyone as much as I thought about her. The only way to truly get over anyone was to find someone else.

Parker paused her packing and spoke into her suitcase, "I don't know." She looked out the window and sent it right back to me.

"What do you want?" she asked. With little hesitation, a response came out from the back of my tongue.

"I want you to be my girlfriend." Mic drop. Even I couldn't believe the candid response. Parker audibly released her breath.

"That's not fair. What do you really want?" She was looking for an out. It's so hard to dive straight in without pulling up at the first sign of danger.

"That is what I want, and I know you have a lot going on but yeah..." I heard myself starting to give her an out. I simultaneously wondered if I was giving myself an out too. Either way, I left her apartment out of the gray. She wasn't ready to call me her boyfriend and that felt personal. I knew it wasn't, but it felt like someone slowly pressed my entire chest into a wall. Now wasn't the right time for her, and I understood that. These talks were never one-and-done, but the space between us widened both emotionally and physically. She was leaving the country for a month and I was back in the red.

12

BROKEN BANANAH

The time to call Parker had arrived. With no privacy in my apartment, I had to utilize what time alone I had. I asked James to go back home and buy time so my mom wouldn't worry about where we were. My saintly elder brother headed off to deliver cleaning supplies as I slowed my hobble. I put my headphones on and paused to take it all in. Scrolling through my contacts, I found Parker right at the top of my recent messages. My body has uncontrollable reactions to certain things and even seeing her name in my phone made my chest jump. I tapped her name and the call screen popped up. No pre-call text, just straight to a phone call. If I was going to do this, I was going to soldier on and do it right. She wouldn't ignore my call. Would she? Whether or not the girl I'm talking to picks up the phone was a huge indicator of how she felt. It's ballsy to call anyone now without texting. It's a ballsy move to call at all. It was more acceptable to video call someone than it was to just ring.

In the hollow of my ear canals, I heard the first dial tone. It reverberated painfully in my brain, sending a clear signal that this was happening. Caller ID made it possible for her to know who it was. There was a time when Caller ID was only for the wealthy. As for now, no turning back. The second ring sounded louder than the first, bringing me closer to reality. My breath got caught up in my throat again and I braced myself for the third ring. Would she pick up?

Time began to freeze as the number of rings increased and voicemail became imminent. In that last second, two thoughts preoccupied my mind. The first was to back out now. It was clear that she didn't want to speak to me. Three rings, that's the threshold, you wait three rings and then you just hang up because after five you go straight to voicemail, and no one makes it out of a voice message better than they did going in. One of my favorite scenes in cinematic history was the scene in *Swingers* where Jon Favreau leaves a series of messages, increasing in cringe-worthy attempts to leave this girl a message... I had gone through ten possible messages in my head between the third and fifth ring. Right at the fifth ring, Parker picked up.

"Ross?" A stalactite from a bat cave seemed to have stabbed right through my chest. Even though my pause lasted no more than a second, it felt like ten.

"Hey Parker."

"You're alive! You all right?"

"Yes, yes. You all right?"

I like that the British ask how someone was by asking them if they're all right. It's almost a direct route to getting straight to the crux of things. Maybe that's the purpose it served, to cut out all the small talk and get straight into what mattered.

I walked down First Ave at the usual geriatric pace in boho sweatpants while leaning on a tropical cane. I had sunglasses on and hadn't shaved in a couple of days. Underneath all that, I toiled around with what I should say. Being honest was tough sometimes. As an adult, I wasn't sure to what extent my lies could actually hold up. Should I just go the whole nine yards and tell her exactly what happened? Should I start off with the little things? If I start with partial truths, will I need to give all the gritty details?

This was our first talk in what felt like forever to me. I had rehearsed how this conversation would go at least twenty times.

"Well, not great to be honest. I'm still a bit rough," I said, deciding to go with the crescendo build-up, but not taking too long to get there.

"Oh no! What happened? Are you all right now? Is everything okay?" she sounded genuinely concerned about me, and I relaxed a bit.

"Yeah everything's fine, thankfully. No complications and all my parts are still attached. Whether they work or not is still up for debate.."

"Oh my gosh! That sounds horrible, but I'm so glad you're alright!" I imagined her in the middle of a business conference, stepping out to take my call and then standing in the middle of a corridor with her left hand on her heart.

"Yeah, me too."

"Is there anything I can do to help at all?"

"Not at the moment. I've got my mom visiting, and James...so everything's covered for the time being," I said. Then the first of many pauses gripped the conversation.

"I was really scared when I saw the timestamp of your email," she said, breaking the silence. She exhaled a deep thought with a gentle subtlety. "You never know what can happen when someone goes under for surgery."

"That's true," I said, nodding even though she couldn't see me. There's another pause and I can hear her breathing. She breaks the silence again.

"Ross, I'm so, so glad you're okay. I mean it." I listen, but also wonder what was the appropriate response to her kindness. "Thank you so much for calling," she said, "and letting me know that you're fine and that the surgery went all right."

"Of course," I said. Another long pause ensues. On the phone, we could have these pauses without the powerful force of eye contact driving the conversation forward.

"Pretty weird," hinting at the elephant in the room, "wouldn't you say?" I had been telling myself that I hadn't done anything wrong. In the court of law, this would not be considered cheating. We, however, were not at the courthouse. I had hurt her, but I also punished her for being dedicated to her work. She was seizing an opportunity to be more than most people could dream of. Had I been driven away by my own jealousy? I didn't believe so, but the inner dialogue got real with me. Parker broke the ice so we could get to the less comfortable situation. We laughed, if only for a moment, for no particular reason.

"Listen," I mumbled, "I just want you to know I'm really sorry."

"Yeah," Parker agreed, "me too." Parker's candid response disarmed me. It doesn't matter how many times a conversation gets rehearsed in my head, that's never how it goes. The bustling streets filled the silence in between our words. In my head, I combed through how to say what I wanted to say. I considered if what I wanted to say had any value in being said. Our conversation carried on in cyclical rounds of how we felt, each with their own sinking truths. These conversations could last hours, and usually did. Talk, listen, understand, argue, defend, manipulate, wait, cry, frustrate, pacify, hang up, text, redial, repeat.

"I can hear your handicap," she noticed, tossing an otherwise comedic statement into the mix. My cane clicked loudly as I walked. My impending arrival back to the apartment provided a logical end to our call. Like a lot of long talks in relationships, no real progress had been made. We said what had to be said in a situation where neither of us was sure how to react. The talk was a necessity. We knew that. I didn't feel good about it, but I felt considerably better than when the conversations were imaginary. Imaginary conversations still continued, but they had more of a basis now. Questions of "what if" lingered. The sinking feeling that I had really blown it also lingered.

"Good luck with your broken dick," Parker playfully said as her salutation.

"Don't be like that." Even if she was being playful, the D word always came off the tongue hard.

"Good luck with your broken," she paused in search of political correctness, "good luck with your broken banana." Her accent elongated the last syllable as though she kept her mouth open when she finished the sentence. Broken bananahhhh. We both laughed enough to hear the nervousness and comedy come out before we giggled a goodbye. The variety of feelings snapping through my brain kept my mind off the pain slowly creeping its way back in. By the time I got up the stairs to my apartment, it was time to take another round of pills.

13

RADIOSHACK

W hen it comes to injuries, people have questions. They float somewhere between "how did it happen" and "are you doing okay." But this was no broken arm. I basically had two routes to take when fielding questions. If you come to personally visit at my apartment, I owned up to the truth. If I got a text or I randomly saw you, you got the bike accident story. For the people qualifying in the former, those usual two questions turned into an unusual five.

Q: What position were you in?

A: Doggy style. This became a question that, the more I answered it, the less it seemed the way it should've happened. This question, more often than not, turned into a future safety discussion. Cowgirl has already been established as the most criminal. Without the proper control, the woman can do both unspeakable good and unstoppable harm. It's no secret that the chances of the woman orgasming increase exponentially in this position. Experts call this a high risk/high reward situation. Traditionally, a man has far more difficulty cumming when he's just laying there. Come to think of it, I guess everyone has a tougher time finishing when just laying there. Interesting. Maybe, subconsciously, our bodies detect danger and can't achieve maximum pleasure on high alert. Probably has something to do with blood flow.

Missionary comes in as the safest for obvious reasons. Unfortunately for a woman (sorry again, women in general), there is the risk of getting jack hammered. For reference, the jackhammer is an involuntary college move that a boy does to a girl when he sees the finish line -- and sprints. Honorary mention has to be awarded to spooking. Spooking is when a couple spoons while also having intercourse. With a nice soft cushion between the parties, it's virtually impossible to misstep.

Q: Did it hurt?

A: It always hurts the first time. It was one of the most painful accidents of my life. I've fractured five bones, had three moles scooped, torn two ligaments, been in two car collisions, and been gashed in the face by a woman's front teeth in a mosh pit that I started at a Fall Out Boy concert. None of those accidents came with an adrenaline rush like this one. After I called 9-1-1 and sat down, I experienced a crippling sensation that permeated my entire body and didn't subside until I got that drip. So yes, it hurt.

Q: Did you finish?

A: No. No! Goodness. The recurrence of this question baffled me. The only thing that came out was blood. Gross, right? Hey, I'm just answering the question. The truth was that it took me longer to finish than the male stereotype. This was not a gift. When Missy Elliott proclaimed that she didn't want "no one-minute man," she left out that she also didn't want no twenty-minute man. She probably wanted somewhere around a ten-minute man, followed by a water break, a nap, and then a movie to play in the background for another nine to ten minutes. The mathematical difference between ten and twenty minutes was nominal on paper, but those ten minutes could have an extreme impact during medium to high intensity physical activity. Again, the answer was no.

Q: Can you have a wet dream with the catheter?

A: Now this was an interesting one that truly highlighted how little I knew about the functionality of the human body. Logic dictated that the answer to this was just as much a 'no' as the previous answer, but my initial reaction wasn't as certain. Using the best one percent of my brain, here's how I'd answer: I was pretty sure that the pee pipe and the jizz pipe were manufactured in different factories. Given this logic, my best guess for wet dreams with the catheter would be 'no,' but you never know until you experience it firsthand, I guess.

Q: Have you talked to Nikki since?

A: Finally one about the girl; the one that served as primary witness to the whole incident. I was all pain and stain, but what about her? After that fateful night, she did stay in touch. She texted me often and sometimes included photos of herself that were as arousing as they were disappointing. With every picture, her butt looked less like a peach and more like a weapon. We didn't have much to talk about, but enough to make pleasant conversation.

Q: How is everything?

A: This one should probably have come first, but the cordial order of medical Q&As didn't exist in this scenario. I was doing okay. Staying positive was tough when everything was status quo, and this was taking its toll. I didn't like doing nothing. I didn't like feeling helpless. I didn't like moving slow. I liked being the one who moved fast and took care of others. As much as I didn't want to admit it, I was having a much tougher time receiving help than I would've, had I been giving it. But I needed it and there weren't any doctors walking into my room anymore. The only doctors that I had spoken to since the break were my uncle, an eye surgeon, and his wife, an anesthesiologist. Talking about any of this with family was more like giving a job update than it was a deviant confession.

Q: Was it worth it?

A: No.

14

THE MIDNIGHT BONER

I t was the best of times. It was the worst of times. Technically, it was a little past midnight, and I awoke to an intense pain shooting through my body. Immediately, my brain pinged various parts to see what the fuck was happening. The pain started in my stomach and ripped through my legs as though I had spent the whole day at the gym. Was yesterday leg day? Irrational explanations flooded my brain. I grabbed my phone, turned on the flashlight, and saw the crimson red of fresh blood. Not good! More irrational thoughts come flooding in. Am I on my period? *Did my penis explode?* Whatever it was, it was not pretty. Amongst the dyed fibers, the flashlight revealed something miraculous sprouting beneath the covers. I was getting my first erection! Well, my first *attempt* at an erection. My Bruce Banner was trying to go Hulk, but found itself restrained by the unrelenting, oppressive catheter tube. It pulled down as my erection tried to pull up. This was not going to work. Blood emanated from the straw that gagged my penis, quickly turning the bed into a bath of horror.

Time to focus. I needed this boner to retreat like it was the Battle of Yorktown, 1781. Red Coat reference aside, I stared at my Phase-2 erection in an attempt to think it into submission.

STAND DOWN! I commanded in my head as stereotypical, unflattering imagery flashed through it. I never knew my grandparents so I couldn't summon their naked bodies for an assist. I thought harder.

STAND DOWN DAMNIT! The problem with thinking about getting rid of an erection was that I also wondered what caused it. Almost immediately, I remembered the sex dream I was having. Ever since my teenage years, I've had a recurring dream about two women seducing me on South Beach. One woman strongly resembled the original hottie, Kelly Kapowski (played by mega babe Tiffany Amber Thiesen) from the 90s' comedy *Saved By the Bell*. She wore a pink string-bikini top and denim cutoffs, top button unbuttoned. The other woman had a mixed skin tone with black, frizzy hair. She wore an open denim jacket that covered her slender figure. They'd always walk towards me in slow motion on the beach, and then we'd get busy down in the sand. Grease reference aside, my two iron ladies had been in my head for years. Some things never change, and they returned with the fury to awaken my midnight boner.

Breathe. Breathe. Breathe. I found alternative use for my meditation practice and it was working. Erector was receding. Like a slug leaving behind a trail as it crawled, blood stained the tube where my penis had previously swallowed. Red tears dripped down the magic mushroom as I reached for the cotton swabs. My brother and mom start to wake up. Great. I continued my breathing, but my superhero tried to hulk itself to a larger version again. For weeks we hadn't been certain Dr. Strangelove would be able to return to full form. I briefly celebrated the half form that fought its way through my dream and into reality. Then reality set back in. My mom and brother, sleeping on my futon, were about to bear witness to the Cotton Massacre.

"STOP!" I verbally commanded my little admiral, gritting through my teeth.

"What's wrong?" My mom had likely already gone to life-or-death situations in her mind. Caught between dousing the fire and explaining the flame, I managed to squeak out that I was fine. I, of course, was not fine.

My immediate priority was to completely lower the tent pole. I inhaled deeply through the nose and exhaled gently through the mouth. For a moment, I'm transported back to grade school years, where every boy struggled to keep down their raging bull. This juxtaposed later in the circle of life when every man struggles to keep it up. *Lion King* reference aside, there were a few ways that middle and high school boys would hide their stiffy (that's what they were called back then). These techniques were necessary mostly when class would end and you'd have to get up, or, even worse, you'd be called up to the front of class. The easiest technique was to use a textbook to cover up. School boys have school books and the best students always kept them on their hip. Personally, that was a sucker's move, too obvious for a sly dog like me. I employed the *uptuck*. I'd reach into my pants, grab my Ron Jeremy, and pull it safely up into my waistband. The blood drained. I remained. The only threat to the uptuck was a surprise hug. Class ends, you give yourself an uptuck, and, of course, Lindsey is waiting right outside the door to give you a squeeze (not *that* kind of squeeze). I'd stick my ass out, hug with my chest, and stroll it off. Even though I had a lifetime of training in mitigating stiffies, nothing prepared me for the urgency I currently faced.

Breathe in, count five, breathe out. Again. Breathe in, count five, breathe out. It was too late. James and my mom stared at the horror.

"Let me get you some water," my mom instinctively said. I cannot emphasize enough how unwanted this situation was where my mom had to help me.

"Mommy, I'm fine. Please." I got defensive in the way anyone does when something's wrong but you want to act like everything's alright. Laying with a half erect penis in the middle of the night was weird for anyone to see, let alone my mother and brother. This was another exercise in humility on the road to recovery.

"You need to drink water," she reinforced as she disappeared into the kitchen. To be fair, drinking water was tough to argue against, regardless of the situation.

"Mommy." I try and freeze her with the single name response. Per usual, it fails.

"Okay, fine." She comes back into my room and places a glass of water on the TV stand. "It's for me," she says. Moments like these are where the phrase 'pick your battles' come from.

"Thank you Mother," I say, invoking her full maternal name like parents use first and middle names. She promptly laid back down, even though I knew she wouldn't be going to sleep anytime soon.

I looked down to find terms of surrender. The troops had, much to delight, retreated. My mom had unintentionally solved the problem. In the midst of her momming, my penis had settled back into its travel size. I surveyed the situation. There was blood on the tube, blood on me, blood on the sheets, and blood on the dance floor. Michael Jackson reference aside, none of those stains mattered. What really mattered was that I received my first erection in ten days. A subtle grin grew across my face as I slipped back into a sleep with one final thought: *it works*.

ALL THE SMALL THINGS

Time was a blur. I woke up uncertain if it was all a dream. Had I had an erection? One glance south confirmed that dream. The dry blood painted onto my catheter meant I needed to shower, which I hadn't tried since coming home. That's because showering, as I knew it, was not the same as it used to be. A traditionally overindulgent past time of the First World, showering had become an only-when-necessary experience. After sink showers had run their course, I was faced with two options in my current state: sponge bath or an attempt at a regular shower. Post Roman-Greek-empire era, sponge baths have lost their sex appeal. When my dad broke his foot and couldn't put pressure on it, my mom and I gave him a sponge bath. When my mom broke her collarbone (a truly shitty experience), my dad and I gave her a sponge bath. Filling the pots from the bath and pouring on the water, soaking the soap and scrubbing away, and trying to maintain the right temperature the whole way. It required patience and love. In India, they scrubbed bronze deity statues with milk as a symbol of surrender and servitude. Surrendering autonomy in the shower humbled anyone, and I could see why it can be somewhat of a ritual. In my family, it was the byproduct of and an exercise in human fragility.

With regular showers a distant luxury, I attempted to stand in the shower on my own. I mostly wanted to control the scrubbing vigor, sensitive to the fact that everything, and I mean *everything*, was connected. On its own, stepping into the shower took thirty seconds per foot. That may not sound like a lot, but statisticians would view that as a 1500% increase in the average entry time. With my mom and brother acting as moving handrails, they somehow managed to get me into a standing position without the water hitting my catheter tube. My mom turned the shower head in my direction and sent a hellfire of water onto me. Like a barrage of rubber bullets, the water droplets hit my catheter and struck a gong that reverberated deep inside my organs. James reached out with a solution. He would hold my pee bag outside of the shower as I quickly washed. With the curtain wide open, I unstrapped my catheter bag and handed it to my brother.

"Go slow, and will you hold it up?" I asked. Not my weirdest little-brother moment, but right up there with the best of them. God bless the responsibility family has when it comes to taking care of their own. I know that every family member goes through these unsung hero moments, but no one likes to see their loved ones struggle. Yet there he was standing next to an open shower, staring at his old-man younger brother trying to clean himself as the water from the shower splashed on them both. Brotherly love.

For all the comfort and joy a shower can bring, this instance added to the few poor experiences I'd had. The other poor experiences were when the water temperature handles were impossible to figure out. With a single knob shower, I'd turn it all the way on and dial it back halfway, getting burned or frozen somewhere in between. If there were two knobs, often unlabeled, I'd have to play mad scientist to find the balance between them. This game of patience would, of course, be played while standing there naked trying to avoid the water. Even when the knobs were right, the amount of time remained a mystery. The assumption that it might take awhile would often end up in third degree burns. The assumption that I should turn the shower on and do something else for a couple minutes while it warmed up was just plain wasteful. And for the record, I don't respect people who brush their teeth in the shower. That's taking the wastefulness of leaving the sink on while you brush and tripling it.

After successfully stepping out of the shower and patting myself dry, I was faced with another problem. I felt my first real urge to go the bathroom. As in, the big one. Anybody that's gone under anesthesia knows that constipation may come knocking and I wasn't having that again. After a lot more cringing and wincing, I settled onto the seat. Going number two after surgery was, like life, all about the balance of when to push and when to wait. I've never found the word poop nor the act of pooping funny, and I've always tried to get it over with as soon as possible. I'm not the type who lingered on the toilet to read a book of endless facts. To me, we are the most vulnerable when we shit. The longer we have our pants down, the more open to attack we are. Dogs are the best example. When they shit, they look scared that someone is going to come and steal their treats, knowing there isn't shit they can do about it until they finish their shit. That's why dogs don't wipe. They're anxious to get back on guard.

After an unsuccessful couple of minutes go by, a universal truth set in. Nothing good comes easy. I think to some extent we are all guilty of literally and figuratively pushing too hard, but the stakes were higher this time around. There are times when, no matter how hard you push, things don't budge and life goes on. This time around, every push reverberated through my body. Everything was connected, and when I'd squeeze my intestine to activate my butt, my penis would squeeze and activate my tube. I could only push so many times before the discomfort outweighed the need to go. At that moment, I knew I was lucky to have never had a hernia. James had a hernia when he was in college, and that surgery was the toughest recovery. Between the two of us, we had enough medical mishaps to cover for a family of ten.

I sat on the throne, reflecting back when bowel movements were easier. I also reflected on my blessings. Even if I couldn't get anything out, I still sat in a bathroom with toilet paper and running water. In my comically small Manhattan apartment bathroom, my knees pressed against the wall. Taking notice of all the small things around me, I pushed and waited with no success. Flashes of prune juice ran through my mind as I reached for my phone. Might as well get comfortable and ride this one out. I never thought of the toilet as a great place to reflect, but there I was. I had become a porcelain philosopher, still wet from my first shower as a 90-year-old man.

16

LESSONS LEARNED, PT 1

While it was true that life could change in the blink of an eye, time could just as easily slow down. That's when there's room for observation and lesson learning. When life is slow, sounds are amplified and minute details are appreciated. It's a state of complete awareness, which the Japanese called Zanshin, and it's what I felt in my new pace of life. After a week and a half of walking step by step, tethered to myself, here's what I had learned.

Lesson One: Staring is Rude. To some extent, we all know this, but it really hits you when you're the one being stared at. Guys are usually not the ones being stared at. I'd go for a walk every day and I was easily the slowest in the herd of New Yorkers. Senior citizens would breeze by, including ones carrying groceries or wheeling a laundry cart. Gray-haired grandparents with little shuffling steps would look back with their judgement. The sound of their black flats scraping against the paved sidewalk were clear as day.

It didn't help that New Yorkers, even the ones over 65, walked faster than the average deer. A study some time back actually revealed that New Yorkers were the eighth fastest walkers in the world. I had always been one of them. I have little to no patience for sidewalk blockers, often fantasizing about stiff arming my way through a four-wide group of people.

And then there was the staring. Not that I could blame any of them. If I saw an unshaven guy in sweats with a small tent in his pants using a cane, arms linked with his mother, calling her Mommy -- I'd look too. In the end, it's okay to look. It's natural. Just don't *stare*.

Lesson Two: The truth is always funnier. When things first started out, I tried to hide my incident with a series of cover-up accidents previously established with my doctor. There was the bicycle accident, where I swerved out of the way of New Yorkers violating the bike lane and was thrown crotch-first into a pole. There was also the simpler version where I fell and broke my leg. In that case, I didn't specify *which* leg, so there was half of a truth in there. I'd fantasize about saying I was attacked. It wasn't cool to be mugged or beat in the city, but it's not something that people interrogated much further on. Fortunately for me, I had never been mugged. I attribute this to having resting terrorist face, which was the Middle Eastern version of resting bitch face for men.

Finally, there was the truth. This was the most satisfying and funniest when dealt in a nonchalant manner. A neighbor in my building saw me in the stairwell, gingerly taking it one step at a time when she earnestly asked what happened. Without thinking I replied, "Oh I broke my penis having sex."

"Are you serious?" She asked as we continued in our opposite directions. I could tell that she really wanted to laugh, but wasn't sure if it was a joke.

"Yup!" I reassured her. We both burst into laughter that echoed through the building, still unsure of the situation. The truth was always funnier.

Lesson Three: Desperation breeds innovation. After a couple of daily walks and multiple stares, I figured there had to be a better way to stabilize the dong show. The more I moved, the more I got tugged. Tugs, even in middle school, were bad. On top of that, my barbed-wire stitches caught onto any fiber they could and pulled on my incision wounds. No me gusta. After taking a little time to sketch a comfortable, effective blueprint, I got to work on my custom dick sling. My design modified the traditional Hanes briefs, affectionately referred to as tighty whities sometimes. Briefs were to white people what wife beaters were to Latinos. Only the people wearing them thought they were okay. The problem was that I couldn't wear briefs like a normal person because they squeezed the unit in too tight. The comfort and utility of cotton snuggling the sack while pressing in the beak usually made briefs valuable, but the beak needed space. To do this, I slit some fabric right under the waistband and down each side of the strike zone. This created a penis window that kept the ball support I wanted, and the airspace I needed. Then, I created a resting pad to prop out my little lion man by placing a generous amount of my tissues on the bottom of the P-window. I'm not talking about the cheap tissues that blow open a shotgun hole when you sneeze. I'm talking about the ultra soft, lotion with aloe and Vitamin E, three-ply tissues. My allergies wouldn't allow for anything less. I also used them when I masturbated, but I learned to sneeze long before I started stroking it so relax. The landing pad was essential to prop the shaft outward. The catheter tube traditionally tugged down, and I wanted to minimize the directional changes that could occur. Facing forward felt much better than whatever direction the wind went.

With my stabilizing runway carefully constructed, I needed to protect my stitches. Since tissues were more expensive than toilet paper, I folded over a small amount of TP to wrap my little baby in. This wasn't some bootleg, public restroom toilet paper either. This was the cotton cloud, ripple technology type that gave my butt a hug after it did its duty/doodie. Two toiletries I stopped skimping on after I got my first job were towels and toilet paper. I didn't want to feel scratchy after a shower, and I definitely didn't want to feel dirty after a poop.

After wrapping my rock star, I slowly lifted the modified briefs over the tube, up the leg, and secured them around my waist. I taped to my leg with a decent amount of slack so a casual two step wouldn't be a problem. With everything in place, I walked around my two hundred square foot apartment space with a new lease on life. After snapping a photo of my architectural achievement, I realized that sometimes you've got to be in a corner to find your way out.

17

WHEN THE LEVEE BREAKS

Sometimes, when I'm feeling philosophical, I sit there and think: how do people *choose* to become urethra reconstruction specialists? Do they go through medical school and then flick through a menu of specializations? Is there a chart of supply and demand? Whatever the case, a good doctor has certain universal qualities. Good doctors are like good partners, except a little more expensive (depending on the partner). They pay attention to you, make you feel like you are the only one in the world, and always make time for you even when they have a fully booked day. Dr. Rajiv met and exceeded the makings of a good doctor.

Dr. Rajiv, also known as my miracle doctor, was the urethra reconstruction specialist that was called in after the first surgeon, Dr. Herm, opened me up. That's because they couldn't tell from the initial tests that I had severed my urethra. Even if you didn't know anatomy, you would agree that a severed urethra might call for a specialty doctor. There weren't that many surgeons that were urethral reconstruction specialists in the country, and Dr. Rajiv happened to be right down the street. Only in New York City would the only doctor you need be down the street. In fact, I was told Dr. Rajiv (aka my savior, aka the man with the magic hands) was one of five doctors in the entire country that specialized in reconstructing pipes. Deus Ex Machina? Absofuckinglutely.

Walking into the doctor's office, I wasn't sure what to expect. There certainly was no one less than forty years older than me, and there were no other men with catheters in. I slowly hobbled to check in. The lady at the desk took the clipboard, examining my name.

"So *you're* Ross," Stacey said in her wonderful and musical Haitian accent. "You caused quite a ruckus in here." She was kind and perfect for easing me into an appointment. She had the type of smile that could make instant friends and that's what I needed with the nerves running around under my skin. That being said, I had no idea what she was talking about.

"I like to keep it exciting, what can I say?" She proceeded to tell me what transpired the morning of my surgery. Dr. Herm opened me up and immediately called for backup. Well, he texted for backup. He took a picture of the carnage and the distress signal worked. After Dr. Rajiv saw the image, he called in his practice to cancel the day's appointments. His entire office scrambled to call patients and rebook them so that he could come operate. My legend of misfortune broke ranks while I lay unconscious on an operating table. Stacey explained that everyone was incredibly accommodating and understanding. If they were patients at a urology office, I guess they knew it could've been them.

When the nurse called my name, I got up to walk in and asked my mom to stay behind. My mom looked at me and shrugged. I was already in a state of suffering and the less I had to fight my mom's level of growing concerns the better. A well dressed man passed me in the hallway and nodded his salutation. I couldn't quite place him in the plethora of memories that followed my accident, but it turns out that he was indeed Dr. Rajiv. At first I wondered how he knew who I was, and then my brain kicked into gear and I realized our initial meeting was one-sided. It's probably not the first time a grown man I don't remember had touched my genitals. Can I say that?

Upon sitting on the traditionally eerie examination chair in the doctor's office, I was greeted by someone who was clearly one of my people. Kate, a tattooed young woman with orange hair, was the physician's assistant. Her orange hair was a tell tale sign that she was probably a theater major. There's something about urology that put us past the small talk. We discussed children first. She didn't want them, and I said I'd be lucky if I made it that far. The pain of going into labor was her sticking point.

"I don't think a man can ever know what a woman goes through when she goes through childbirth."

"To be fair, this," I said, pointing at my crotch, "this might be the closest thing." She agreed. Women who don't want children feel the need to justify why. If you don't want something that you don't have to have, that seems perfectly fine by me. A guy friend of mine wanted to do his part in overpopulation by keeping his swimmers at bay. He had a full study prepared, and I was like "Hey man, I'm not mad." There should be a dating app for people with deal breakers or absolutes. Smoking, cats, and kids weren't for everybody. The first two definitely weren't for me.

"Can you imagine the intensity of the pain during labor? It's contraction after contraction and then you push and push and push until you can't push anymore. You're exhausted, but you've got to keep pushing, but no matter how hard you keep pushing, this little alien won't come out. You're laying there screaming your head off while everyone else screams 'BREATHE' into your vagina until finally this thing ten times the size of said vagina breaks your hips and emerges in a sea of goo. Just isn't my thing."

"Well hey," struggling to find a neutral statement to progress the conversation, "different strokes for different folks." I imagine my PR will be similar if I ever have a daughter and she tells me that she just had her first period.

"Oh yeah, and then you've got all sorts of complications as a woman if you weren't planning on being pregnant. A man knocks you up and you've got to decide whether or not you want to keep the baby." She wasn't done. "Abortion's taboo, which I get. You're freaking out because it's like you know you're not ready for that responsibility or the shame, but at the same time you feel like maybe this is my calling. Like when someone tells you they've enrolled you in grad school. For men it's as easy as walking out the door. Literally." She lost me on the grad school part, but I followed almost everything else. The key thing in any of these conversations was that we all had different life experiences and we have to understand that, even if we don't agree with someone, doesn't mean we have to disagree with them. Casually dropping abortion five minutes after meeting someone could go nuclear in some parts of the world, but I like that she took the understanding route rather than the heavily opinionated route. You never know how you'll act until it's you.

"If it's any consolation," I said, "I might not even have the choice of kids."

"Wait, hold on, what do you mean you're not going to have the choice?"

"Well, after the first exam, the doctor kind of said that, in the worst case scenario, I might not be able to have kids."

"Oh," she backpedaled, "I mean, I think that's a bit dramatic, but do you want to have kids?"

"Someday, yeah," I said.

———

Medical instruments were expensive and, thus, didn't get replaced often. Kate helped me into a blue gown and placed me onto a table that looked like it was ironically tailor-made for a woman giving birth. Two individual leg rests, each with inner thigh pads, spread my eagle. My penis dangled in the middle while my balls rested on the porch. Women must sit on these at the OBGYN, which I always remembered the letters for but had no clue what they stood for. The doctor came in and flashed a smile as I sat there, open for business. We shook hands, which I appreciated. Some doctors don't do that anymore because of germs, but he had already touched me in worse places.

"The legend! How are you?" I was genuinely excited to meet this man. He took my admiration in stride, simply nodding away the well-deserved cheers. At the same time, I'm sure he sensed my anxiety at this crucial two-week mark after surgery. Good doctors have a serenity to them that put a patient at ease. Dr. Rajiv carried this serenity.

"I'm fine," he laughed, looking through some notes. "How are you feeling?"

"Top of the world," I said, pulling off my biggest smile. "Time to look at your handiwork, I guess." He waved a hand carelessly as though he fixed urethras in his sleep.

"It was an interesting call to get, but you're young and healthy. Any discomfort with the catheter?" I laughed at this obviously rhetorical question.

"Does anyone *not* experience discomfort with a catheter?" He joined in on the laugher. I wasn't going to let him be too professional. If the banana boat was going to sink, I wanted to be smiling on the way down. The hybrid room we were in served as both a consultation and operation space. It was a decent size with a giant processing machine on one wall, a massive x-ray machine right beside me, and fluorescent lights bearing down from above. My pupils adjusted to their surroundings as they caught a tray of tools being slowly wheeled to my birthing chair.

"Okay, I'm going to fill your bladder up with this dyed fluid until it's completely full." Dr. Rajiv had connected my catheter tube to another bag of solution. This reverse-pee injection system looked like an experiment from a sci-fi dystopia. With a subtle squeeze of the solution bag, Kate began the proceedings. We take peeing for granted. There's no thought process other than the occasional focus it takes in a public restroom or the great outdoors. It's natural. Emptying the bladder was a mindless miracle where our bodies became a bilge pump. In my case, it was like a movie in reverse. Rather than emptying the bladder, it was gradually being filled up. This created a super bloated feeling as if a balloon was expanding inside my lower intestine.

"Whoa!" I couldn't help but exclaim as they injected the dye into me.

"Do you feel full?" the doctor asked.

"Full is questionable. I feel weird is what I feel," I said, rearranging the English language on the fly.

"That's to be expected. I need you to feel uncontrollably full, like you absolutely have to urinate."

"Well, I definitely feel like I have to pee?" I questioned.

"Do you *really* need to? You're going to want to be absolutely full." Dr. Rajiv insisted, even though his congeniality made it tough to take his ask too seriously. Then again, everything that was happening was tough to take seriously.

"The way you're saying it makes me question if my definition of full is the same as yours, but I definitely feel the pressure."

"Okay, we're gonna do a little bit more just in case, I think we're nearly there…"

"Oof, do you have a tank meter on any of those machines?" I joke, taking small breaths. Kate looked back at the doc, clearly preparing for the next step. People in the medical field have their own signals so us civilians don't freak out when something's about to go down. They weren't fooling me. I saw that look. Something was about to go down.

"Kate, let's go ahead and remove the Foley," Dr. Rajiv instructed Kate in the gentlest way. Right when the discomfort hit its maximum, Kate pulled the Foley out.

SSSSSSSSHHHHHHEEEEEEEEEEEEEIIIIIIITTTTTT

My nose wrinkled and my teeth clenched as I sucked in air. It felt like somebody pulled a tweed rope through five feet of my internal lining. Coming back to the whole numbing thing, I realized that they didn't actually inject any of it into my penis, just around the tip, but, at that point of my life, I couldn't tell one from the other. The actual numbing injection had not yet begun.

"Are you in pain?" The miracle doctor asked, putting a

reassuring hand on my shoulder. This, for sure, was another rhetorical question.

"I think I'm in the expected amount of pain for having something pulled out of you, that's for sure." I looked up into his friendly face; genuine concern etched between his brows. That's when the giant x-ray machine came into use. I was instructed to turn on my side and pee. This instruction alone was elementary on paper, but I knew it would be no small task, given the current situation. They needed me to pee so that the x-ray machine could take pictures and inspect my urethra's healing progress. While this makes sense, I hadn't used my bladder in two weeks. Like any muscle that you haven't used in a while, it takes a second to shake the dust off. So there I was in the fetal position with a giant machine pointed at my little machine while Dr. Rajiv and Kate encouraged me to go.

"Stage fright is a real thing," I offered as a delay tactic. They gave me the courtesy laugh but clearly wanted the show to go on.

"It's okay, you're doing fine." I never thought I'd need urination encouragement in my life, let alone in my 20s. For now, I had to summon every ounce of willpower imaginable to do it. I broke a sweat and closed my eyes. I took a deep breath and braced myself. Flashbacks came to mind of all the times I was in an empty public bathroom and yet someone saddled up in the urinal next to mine. *COME ON DAMNIT!* I may have stopped using my bladder, but I still had heart. Desperate to flow, I searched for the trigger. I squeezed, tensing up every muscle. I wanted to force that piss out of me. My internal voice yelled even louder.

COME ON DAMNIT!

And then, it happened. I got a drip! The x-ray machine clicked as I pushed another drop. I kept pushing and pushing, trying to tap the well for more as my medical cheerleaders hoped from the sidelines. And then, it stopped happening. The hose closed. Glaring down with absolute intention, my eyes watched the disappointment grow around the room. Muscle memory hadn't fully returned. Dr. Rajiv floated over to comfort me.

"This is normal. Your bladder has been getting a lot of rest," he said, "but we're going to need more." In what can only be called yet another that's-what-she-said moment, I bit my tongue and focused. My surgeon turned P.E. coach stepped back to let me focus. This must be what erectile dysfunction felt like, which I had yet to experience. Actually, that's not true. My first college girlfriend and taker-of-my-virginity lived three hours away from me. She went to school at Florida State University, while I went to its rival school, University of Florida, making us the Romeo and Juliet of college couples. We missed one another so much that we each drove halfway across the state during the week (!) for one night of pure steam. After checking into a Days Inn, we jumped onto the crusty bed and furiously made out. Alas, no boner to be found. When my engines didn't kick in, I did what any guy in that situation did, I performed oral sex on her. "Performed oral sex" is a funny phrase for it, but as a theatre kid, I feel it's rightfully appropriate. My *oral performance* neared its curtain call as my lovely girlfriend, Lane, went to reciprocate. Instead of a rocket booster, she found a dead rooster. My penis balloon lay limp, bereft of air. We each took turns flopping it around, trying to wake him up.

"We're going to need more," Lane and I thought in unison, staring into the eye of the tiger. Despite our best efforts, my springbox had malfunctioned. She, being loving and kind hearted, didn't make me feel bad for the teenage letdown. After dinner around the rest stop, we went back to our hotel room and broke up. No we didn't. We went back and had great college sex! But neither of us ever forgot the day the sun forgot to rise.

———

Back in the doctor's office, my focus reached peak intensity. And then, I felt it coming. Like the dew sweating off a morning apple, another delightful drip dropped out. Success! I had pulled the sword from the stone. Only this time, I knew there was a serious surge not too far behind. A warm sensation of urine dribbled across my body as I lay on my side. A montage of streams and gushing rivers ran through my mind. This was the pee we'd been looking for. I was quite literally peeing on myself as the crowd rejoiced. My radiation gown protected me from the harmful x-rays as well as the overflow making its ways across the room. The steady drips I started with minutes prior had grown into a full stream. The pee pad they placed under me (yes, they placed a doggy pee pad under me) was earning its keep. Dr. Rajiv snapped the x-rays and encouraged me to finish.

"Okay that's plenty, thank you Ross." It's hard to close a door once it's swung too far open. I stared at the water works, begging them to stop. As though to employ the Force, I squinted my eyes and somehow the faucet turned off. My ceremonial first pee wasn't pretty, but it was done. Over the next thirty seconds, I watched Dr. Rajiv examine the images of my urethra being aptly displayed on a tiny monitor. Generally speaking, good news comes quicker than bad news. He paused before dictating medical jargon to Kate, double checking his own calculations. I heard a sigh as he turned to deliver the news.

"Well, it appears that your urethra," his low tone foreshadowing bad news, "has a very small amount of leakage and has not fully healed." I could somehow see it coming, mostly by nature of Murphy's Law and its general role in my life. For this reason, I avoid WebMD so my brain doesn't manifest any 'what-if' scenarios. Dr. Rajiv normalized the news with positive notes on my progress. It's hard to pay attention in a doctor's office even though that's the one place we should always be paying absolute attention.

"Let's first take a look, but we're going to have to put a catheter back," the doctor said. "Kate, can you prep the syringe with..." I blinked my eyes wide open. Catheter? Syringe? The last time I saw a syringe was at Señor Frog's, and they filled it with red jello. Kate produced a similar syringe with fillings that weren't meant for my mouth. It contained gel that would numb the lining of my urethra for the camera they would insert into my penis. This was the same camera the doctors at the hospital used for a prolonged amount of time the last time. Cystoscopy was a familiar foe. Kate took a commanding grip of my limp dick, which I say in the most literal and non demeaning sense, and matched its tip to the tip of the plastic syringe. Face to face, they kissed for a brief moment before Kate emptied the clip. The gel slowly moved into me. My penis was slowly drinking the gel like a baby being fed the bottle. Some of it escaped out of the tip as the supply struggled to meet the demand. It was gross but also pretty hilarious. Like watching myself shotgun a beer, too much moved too fast from one container to the other. Unlike myself shotgunning a beer, the slow-motion pace allowed me to take out my phone and record video. Dr. Rajiv and Kate had become accustomed to my antics at this point, and I probably would've recorded more had I been coherent for the previous procedures.

Dr. Rajiv stepped up to the plate with his long, thin black camera in one hand and my spaniel ear in the other. With little warning, he pushed the snake-like camera into my snake-like penis. WOOP! My whole body tensed up, but I knew better than to squirm. The inside of my urethra suddenly appeared on the TV screen opposite us. Although it was the inside of my body, watching the livestream was truly an out-of-body experience. All those times at the science center where I would walk through life-sized body exhibits were oddly accurate.

"Yes, you can see right there," Dr. Rajiv said pointing at the screen, "the little issue we've still got."

"Yeah, fuck. That's tiny." I was rightfully let down that something so small could be that big. I continued asking obvious questions. "So what does this mean?"

"It means that we're going to have to put the catheter back," he said, "for another two weeks."

Two weeks… *Fuck.* I was no mathematician, but that was doubling my tube time.

One much bigger thing came to mind when the doctor said two

weeks: my best friend's destination wedding was in one week, and I was the best man. The timing was all supposed to work out so that I would be healed from the initial predicted recovery time. The last thing I wanted to do was explain to his wedding party why I was attached to a bag. All of that didn't matter as Kate prepared the new catheter.

If pulling the catheter out was like tugging out a rope, then putting it back in was like unloading a flamethrower into my urethra. I was unconscious when they inserted the catheter the first time because of the surgery. Being unconscious was a luxury I didn't realize I had. With one quick thrust, Kate pushed the Foley into me as my eyes popped open. I released my unmistakable pain noise followed by heavy breaths, quickly acknowledging that I was okay. The examination room felt like a time chamber. How long had I been in there? Luckily, the endurance check up was over. I had my marching orders for the next two weeks. The good news was that the healing was going well, and the doctor was delighted with my progress. Most importantly, he was pleased with my erections. That made two of us.

I walked out of the room accompanied by my familiar catheter, which my mom immediately noticed. I beat her to saying anything negative.

"Two more weeks with it in, then everything will be fully healed."

"Two more weeks?" She worried, because that's what mom's do.

"Yes, but everything is doing well and the doctor's very happy with my erections." Saying this was weird, but, because of her neverending concern for grandchildren, I said it. "Let's go to lunch and celebrate."

After lunch, we climbed into a taxi to go back home and I realized my wallet was gone. It had fallen out of my sweatpants somewhere between the doctor's office and the restaurant. This was a bit of a fuck-you moment from the universe to me. I've gotten a lot of these little moments throughout my life, and sometimes they add up. I felt my throat clamp down and my eyes well up. This was not the straw that broke the camel's back, but enough wheat to push my brain into a momentary place of negativity. Whether it was watching the subway door close right as I'd get to the train, a stranger unapologetically bumping into me, or a Word document shutting down before being saved, sometimes the little shit set a fire off that made my chest TIGHT.

Why me, man. Fuck this shit.

I sat silently with my sunglasses on and pacified my own moment in the sun. The last thing to do when panicking was to exacerbate the situation. I knew the fury would pass, and if there was one question I didn't want to hear when I was on edge, it was "what's wrong?"

MILE HIGH PEANUTS

I f I strained my eardrums enough, I could hear the bells of love ringing from far, far away. Wedding fever was in the air and I was excited to watch my best friend get married, catheter or not. The ceremony was due to take place in Florida, and that meant two things: packing and figuring out who was going to fill in as caretaker since my mom had gone home. That friend for me was Pat, my other best friend. He was one of the nicest, most caring guys on the planet. He was a tall, built, Haitian guy with dazzling white teeth. And I don't use the term dazzling lightly. Pat brushed his teeth four times a day, which was an absolute reflection of his personality. To top it off, he was an over-the-top, flamboyant character that entertained everyone with his dramatics. He could make anyone, anywhere his friend. He arrived at my apartment all smiles and in full manager mode.

"Ross! You look great! How you holding up?" There was an exclamation mark at the end of all his sentences. It's just how he spoke.

"I'm good baby, you ready?" I said. He clapped his hands and rubbed them together as though to prep for a small jazz routine.

"Alright, let's get the show on the road, how can I help?"

His first task was to help dress me, which was a strong distinction from helping me dress. This wasn't something two friends should be doing for another fifty years. After emerging from a thorough and careful shower, I dried off and retooled my custom sling. That sling may have been funny to look at, but it sure came in handy when I needed it. Pat started dressing me by carefully putting my socks on. I felt pretty helpless. It's one thing when family was helping. It's another thought process to see one of your friends, even someone you've known for 10 years, put your pants on for you. As Pat carefully pulled the elastic waistband of my sweatpants, he paused at eye-level with my penis and looked up at me with the most serious face he could muster.

"If you *ever* say some shit about this," he said, pausing for effect, "I'm gonna motha fuckin *KILL* YOU!" Despite our best efforts not to giggle, we both erupted in laughter. It didn't help that a full length mirror acted like a TV screen for us to see the full hilarity of our actions. What a fucking weird life we were living.

All packed and ready to go, we made it down the stairs and out onto the streets. For the first time in awhile, I was really smiling. Having one best friend by my side on our way to see our other best friend's big day had me feeling pretty lucky. If it's any indicator, the t-shirt I was wearing on the way to the airport read "Don't Worry, Be Yoncé." I stood there leaning on my now famous tropical cane, with a travel pillow strapped around my neck, and my sunglasses on to complete the look. Pat managed to snap a selfie with me lingering in the background and uploaded it immediately. The reaction on Facebook was pretty normal. Everyone assumed that I, in my medical chic getup, was being my normal, not-so-normal self.

We promptly arrived to the airport and Pat was kind enough to grab me a wheelchair. We scooted to the front of the security line, fielding more judging stares than women in heels at 7am. If I saw a guy like me cutting the line in a wheelchair, I would also be mumbling "this guy" to my neighbors. The security guy, whose name tag read Tony, asked me to take my shoes off. I looked at him with a real good *fuck you* look, since this wasn't the easiest task for someone in my position. The airport security line is a real *fuck you* experience regardless of someone's medical condition.

"I'll do it," Pat said, with a real *fuck you*-guy tone. Pat took my shoes off for me as Tony watched. Then, big Tony asked me to put my arms out so he could get a feel. As expected, his hand felt the tube on my leg and his face turned into a combination of fear and wonder. I could feel his fingers frantically fidget as a rush of adrenaline pumped through his body.

"Is this..." he started to ask, looking skittish and feeling around the tube. Noticing the plastic bag attached to my leg, he completes his question, "What *is* this?"

"It's a bag of urine," I said in a matter-of-fact sort of way. "A bag of *my* urine," I completed, as though it was an everyday occurrence in the wild world of airport security. Naturally, he did not seem entirely convinced until he felt more of the tube through my sweatpants. His eyes, popping wide open, signaled even more confusion.

"It's connected to my catheter," I said, looking up to find him without a clue as to what that meant. "It's a tube that goes into my penis because I can't urinate on my own." I stretched out my pants to give him a look, which he only needed a glance of. That registered real quick as his mouth opened to blurt out an apology.

"I'm sorry buddy, go right ahead." I wasn't his buddy, but I nodded my head and sat back in my wheelchair, waiting for Pat to push me on through to the gates. I didn't like airport security for a lot of reasons. It reminded me of the lingering effects of terrorism, which was a weird thought to have. Ultimately, extensive airport security existed because of terrorism, and security companies profited millions by selling more and more invasive screenings. To add to that, there were always people frustrated by the new rules, and what they couldn't take on. There were also always people that still didn't understand when to take off their shoes or remove their devices. People complained about each other on both sides of the line, adding to the misery of the experience. I wasn't sure if I didn't like airport security, or I didn't like people.

After a short wait outside our boarding gate, we finally got onto the aircraft. Airplanes were all about free peanuts, a full can of ginger ale, and the slightest chance of hooking up with a stewardess. As Pat and I made our way to the back of the plane, we befriended the flight attendants, who were already laughing at our roadshow.

"I like your shirt," she said, as I fantasized about the mile-high club. The mind goes where it wants, not where it should. I don't know if she was flirting with me, but the fact that I couldn't do anything, even if given the chance, either increased the playful banter or made me an old-man creeper. At that moment, I felt like we were flirting as she brought me the water we'd requested. Some might say she got paid to smile at people and hand them treats, but delusions were mandatory during this rebuilding phase. Regardless, I reached into my backpack and pulled out an infamous orange pill container. Studies have shown a 65% success rate in opening these containers on the first attempt.

Push in. Turn clockwise... which way is clockwise? Nope, other way.

Why isn't this working? Push in... do I need to push harder? Maybe more of a press. Ok press in down against... yup... and turn.

After cracking the riddle on how to open it, I tilted the container with the intention of pouring only two pills into my hand. I, of course, got six. After putting two pills in my mouth, the dance had begun. Pushing them to the back of my tongue, the pills went loop de loop until I finally got them to the back of my tongue. A sip of water entered my mouth, temporarily displacing the pills I had worked so hard to settle in the back. In order to execute the final swallow, I needed the pills to report to the back of my tongue again. I switched from one cheek to the other, angling my head to get it just right, and then paused. I stalled one last time before giving the final order, and, when the perfect balance of pill placement and mental preparation strike, I gulp. The water swept the pills from the base of my tongue, sending all the players down the hatch. For some, taking pills was an automated sequence. For me, it's a meticulous process that I dread every time. Pat snickered, prompting me to glance in his direction.

"What?" I asked Pat as I took another large drink of water.

"What are you doing?" he asked, doubling up in laughter, clutching his belly. I shrugged.

"Taking my pills. What?" It didn't matter what I was saying because Pat was laughing so hard he couldn't hear me. He rocked back and forth, only popping up to imitate what he'd just seen, and then keel back over in laughter.

"You take *so long* man, what was that?" he said between laughter, "I'm dying! I'm dead bro." Pat imitating me was funny, and if he was being accurate, I guess my process was a bit odd. I haven't really taken pills in front of a lot of people. You don't know about your idiosyncratic tendencies until somebody else points them out. At the end of the day, I didn't want to choke and die on tiny little capsules getting stuck in my throat.

About 18 years prior, I developed a fear of choking at my aunt's house in New Jersey. Christmas morning arrived, and Santa brought my brother jelly beans for his stocking. Everyone knew that jelly beans were, even at base level, a risky candy. While some elite kids received jelly beans in a box with descriptive annotations, most kids received jelly beans in a bag of mystery flavors and, likewise, mixed emotions. Is this yellow a lemon tart or buttery popcorn? Is this red one cinnamon or apple? Is this green one watermelon or, much worse, jalapeño? Jelly beans were a high risk/high reward candy. That risk never had higher stakes than on Christmas morning when my brother James, God bless him, choked on one of those candied devil beans.

My aunt's house turned into an absolute war zone the moment James tried to swallow. Shortly after the botched attempt, he reached for my arm and squeezed. I looked at him, eyes stricken with panic, yelled at the top of my lungs.

"MOMMY!" Like the bat signal beaming from my mouth, everyone was alerted to the danger. All I could hear from my brother, now with the other hand around his throat, was a heavy wheeze. My mom had already appeared, assessed the situation, and summoned my dad. Within seconds, my dad appeared out of nowhere, loaded with maximum alpha energy. All dads had a list of superhero moments, and this was another to add to his. Unlike the time he saved me from the burning gasoline, I got a courtside seat to my dad going full flex. Like a lightning bolt, he shot into the middle of the family room.

"Call 911 now!" he directed at my mom. By the time I looked back, my brother was upside down in my father's grasp. My brother's foot firmly in one of my dad's hands while my brother's head floated inches above the floor. My dad's other hand cocked up, as if to bitch slap someone into orbit, and swung down into my brother's back. *WHACK!* I could hear the thunder inside his chest ring.

"COME ON DAMNIT!" He yelled, as though to scare the devil bean out of him. James dangled as hysteria ensued around the beautifully lit Christmas tree. The ornaments watched in horror. The angels held hands. Sweet baby Jesus hung from the pine, unable to save anyone. The only man that could save us now was my dad. Mariah Carey's "All I Want for Christmas" played in the background, haunting the room with her jingle as everyone reached for air. Was this how it ended? One jelly bean with no known flavor and no known motive? Not on my dad's watch. He yelled a myriad of foreign curse words to the heavens and raised his open palm to the sky.

WHACK!

A light red dot popped onto the floor as time stood still. The silence broke with one fragile cough from James. My dad placed his firstborn gently onto the floor, breathing heavily into his own chest like a beast that had unexpectedly transformed under a full moon. Mariah continued to sing. Jesus and all the angels smiled.

He was breathing. My mom, still crying, hung up the phone and joined the rest of us on the floor next to my brother.

"He's okay," my dad said. And he was. Rolling onto his side, James took deep breaths as he marked off one of his nine lives. From that day on, I never trusted jelly beans again and, likewise, I've never trusted pills to safely travel down my throat.

——

Back on the plane, there was plenty of turbulence en route to Florida that sent the plane into spasm. I, meanwhile, was getting my flirt on with the flight attendants. In my younger days, I thought that having sex with a stewardess on a plane would be tops. In my older days, I think that would still be awesome, but what I really wanted was a buddy pass. I'm not saying one would lead to the other, but the chances had to increase at least a little.

Eventually the flight attendants disappeared in front of that literal and figurative first class curtain, and I had to find another way to entertain myself. I scanned the plane to see what kind of creatures I was sharing this rocket with. While picking my nose, I noticed an attractive woman. On the third second of looking, she looked right at me looking right at her. I tried to play it off by digging deeper into my nose. How do people sense when they're being looked at? Why do we have to look more than a moment? With no way out of this embarrassing moment, I closed my eyes and dove into an ugly, mouth open, economy class sleep.

We finally touched down at our destination and waited to deboard until everyone else was off. There was supposed to be a wheelchair waiting for me as we exited, but there was not. We anxiously waited, trying to figure out how we were going to make our connection when an old lady came up from behind us with a wheelchair.

"Is there anyone else on the plane?" she asked in a frail voice.

"No ma'am, we're the last ones off," I said.

"Well this chair was supposed to be for somebody in there. I guess it's for you?" she half offered, skeptical of someone with a full head of hair needing a wheelchair. I sat down and the old lady, already wheezing for air, began pushing the chair up the sky bridge. It didn't take long to realize she wasn't strong enough for the job, but what was I going to say? Pat had gone ahead to check our gate while I was left alone with Wonder Woman. She had managed to get me about six feet up the subtle incline when we stopped moving forward.

"Um, Pat…" I called out with a small sense of urgency. I felt the wheelchair move slightly backwards. The call for Pat increased and so did the speed at which I moved helplessly backwards down the gate ramp. Pat spotted us and leapt down the runway, stopping me from rolling onto the tarmac. In an everyday hero moment, he took the reins from this fragile woman and pushed me in the right direction.

"Excuse me, sir!" the old lady said, clearly out of breath. It was too late. Pat and I were zipping through the airport *Grand Theft Auto* style to catch our connecting flight. Short on time and needing to go up a level to get to our new terminal, we cut through a line of handicapped folks who were all waiting to ride the same shaft. Excusing ourselves constantly among the crowd, we weaved our way through the glances to pack into the elevator. Four senior citizens and their caretakers, plus Pat and myself occupied every square inch of this car. Music would have helped the silence of our temporary home, but instead we just said hello to everyone with a smile to acknowledge that one of us was not like the others. As we looked around, we were greeted by a familiar smile.

"You two again?" It was the stewardess that liked my shirt. Bingo.

"Please stop following us," I started.

"Okay this guy," Pat interjected, "we are hopefully going to catch our flight." The stewardess flashed her smile as though to reveal a secret.

"I already let them know to wait for you." Pat and I gave her the universal look of gratitude, and then exchanged looks. It paid to be nice, even if there was no buddy pass involved.

We arrived to our connecting flight without a problem and hobbled onto the second plane. It was smaller, and smaller unfortunately wasn't better, but it got the job done. There was a baby two rows behind us, but I had no room to complain about other passengers. I popped on my noise-cancelling headphones, which were worth their weight in gold when babies were around, and settled in. When the plane finally landed, the familiar feeling of Florida humidity wrapped us all around. We were home, and the fun was just getting started.

19

CRUISING ALTITUDE

Florida. Land of swamp people, retirees, and everyone I went to grade school with that didn't make it out. I breathed in the hot air, closed my eyes, and thought of how lucky I was to be alive. There was always a bit of nostalgia in my home state. My childhood memories were similar to most middle class suburban kids. I played sports, did my homework, and worked at a handful of side jobs. The smaller jobs included selling golf balls, tearing tickets, driving a promotional truck, landscaping, and playing music. At my main job, I worked as a waiter in the restaurant of an upscale retirement community named Village on the Green. The same clientele ate there on most nights, and the only reason residents stopped eating there was if they stopped eating in general. I learned a lot from that job, but mostly I learned that senior citizens drank *a lot*. One couple, a woman and her wheelchair-bound husband, came in laced off of Dewar's every Friday. At the ripe age of 16, I couldn't serve them alcohol so the wife would go to the bar for refills. One special night, the wife had gotten up when the husband decided he couldn't wait. He reached across the table to take her drank as I watched from the alcove. The man's reach wasn't enough and what happened next can only be described as a real life promo for sobriety. His wheelchair started to tip as I darted towards his table, but it was too late. I swooped under to keep wheelchair from becoming horizontal. His wife appeared, and the husband immediately grabbed her arm, slowly dragging us all to the ground. So there I was under two senior citizens, drunk in love, wondering if this was what I had to look forward to.

———

Pat got our luggage and we headed off to the wedding venue. Weddings have always been a wild card event, with so many details that can go wrong. The food, number of diverse people, relatives meeting, the single crowd, the music, and the speeches were all different bits that could send everything south. It's amazing anyone got through them together. For some couples, weddings were an all out celebration. For others, it was the final test they'd face before earning a tax break and a certificate of participation.

I didn't want to distract from the celebration with my condition, but it was going to be tough if the real story got out. This would be determined by who could figure it out, and who could we could convince with the bike story. It didn't take long for the questioning to begin. My friend's husband Tyrell, a doctor, made a beeline for us from the poolside bar. Tyrell was two beers in, but that's all he needed.

"Hey guys, good to see you both!" He said. Without skipping a beat, he leaned in and whispered, "Alright, so what really happened?"

Pat and I exchanged glances. The bike story would do no good here, even if he was primarily in the natal ward. His eyes popped out of his head when I told him what happened. Medical professionals have all the smart questions with proper names for body parts that I could barely keep up with. He wasn't the only healthcare provider there either. The bride's aunt, Darcy, also happened to be one.

"How are you holding up dear?" she asked after coming over to greet me.

"Better, thank you," I jubilantly replied.

"So what exactly happened again?" She baited. "Somebody mentioned an accident." I looked into her eyes and prepared to deliver my false tale. As I stumbled over my opener, the bride interrupted.

"She used to be a nurse. She already knows. Nice try, Auntie." I darted a look her way for trying to get me, and all she could do was smile back for getting caught. She went into her purse and pulled out a bag of pills. There are two types of pill people. Ones that have the days-of-the-week box, and ones that have the mixed bag. Aunt Darcy had the mixed bag. As she sifted through, I played out my inevitable options. When (not if) she handed me something to take, did I do it? Did I pass? We're all guilty of ingesting things we weren't sure of, even after we've read the label.

"This is the real stuff," Aunt Darcy said in her most innocent drug dealer tone. They were painkillers, she explained, that I might want with all the movement I'd be doing. She was right. I'd moved more in the past 24 hours than I had in the past two weeks, enduring more tugs and discomfort than I'd hoped. I accepted the pills and listened to her advice on when to take them, including the ones that we immediately took together. For a moment, teenage versions of ourselves appeared to share this deviant moment, even though we were full-sized, freewill adults. Retreating back to the men's house, I wondered how soon and how hard the effects would hit.

Three hours later, I woke up on a couch with all the groomsmen putting their tuxedos on. Women don't have to buy a tuxedo. Instead, they have to buy a dress that they'll never wear again, and probably don't look good in. Men get to wear tuxedos. The only choice here was whether to buy or rent. Diego insisted that we bought a tux, claiming that it'd be worth the investment if we wore it more than once after the wedding. We also went to the shop together and my desire for Diego's happiness superseded my will to be cheap. After a quaint fitting and $800, I bought my first tux from Hugo Boss, the white man's gateway drug into formalwear. Two months later, it was finally time to put it on.

We started with the bottoms. With two grown men kneeling at each leg, the careful task of putting my pants on began. When I ordered the tux, it was safe to say there was a smaller bulge in my pants. Diego and Pat pulled one side up at a time as they tried not to disturb the piece in between my legs. With every tap on the catheter, I'd grit my teeth and suck in hard.

"If you could just turn a little sideways," Pat methodically instructed, "we can slip this over here." Diego's two rotund uncles stood by my side, each holding an elbow. Pat had them lift me up like two bouncers booting a douchebag at the end of the night.

"I think he'll have to step into it from a different angle, so it doesn't ride up his crotch," Diego suggested, getting in on the fun. It took a while to figure out the dynamics of getting my pants on with minimal discomfort. They dipped me in and out of my pants like a strawberry in chocolate. This wasn't fun, but it was funny as hell. I honestly just wanted to get my fucking pants on. Then, right as the boys emptied a bottle of cinnamon whiskey, the waistband on mis pantalones clicked around my hips. Success.

After all the less challenging pieces came together, it was time for the last and hardest piece: the bow tie. For the next thirty minutes, we attempted over and over again. There's a reason why bow ties aren't as popular as ties. They're impossible to get right. With each of us watching a different tutorial online, the race to finish was on. The length was challenging to get right, but tightening the loop was where we kept messing up. Pat finished first and had no clue what he'd done to make it work. He attempted to do that thing that dads do where they stand behind you and tie your tie. It didn't work. After bowing my fingers in and out of various holes, I finally got it right.

Pictures before the wedding are almost as important as the wedding itself. Skimp on the food, the flowers and the invitations, but don't let your Uncle be the photographer. When I started my career behind the camera, I shot free engagement sessions from Craiglist, an online classified board. While gaining experience, I quickly learned the nightmare of the wedding business. The free nature of these sessions also brought out a certain type of couple, and one particularly rural session kept me from coming back. The woman, a force in her own right, showed up with two kids, and the man showed up in tinted sunglasses from 7-Eleven. When she took a break from barking at her fiance to remove the sunglasses, I asked the woman about the kids.

"They are both mine, natural births thank you."

Vital information, thank you.

"This little angel, say hi Melanie, is from my previous relationship, and this little guy is between the two of us," she turned her glance from the child and glared at her future husband. "His name is *Justice*." The lasers from her eyes almost broke my camera.

When people ask me to how much to spend on a wedding photographer, I remind them that they only get one shot to capture the moment. The only work around is that the wedding party is a handful of actors ready to take the stage for a posed candid. I am, of course, teeing myself up here. Before we got to groomsman pictures, Pat and I hobbled to this beautiful little chapel that we weren't using for the ceremony. As a joke, we posed at the door with our hands in one anothers and took a picture as though we'd eloped. We posted it with the caption "Twist" and the wedding hashtag (which was a relatively new concept). In no time at all, the internet was on fire.

My mom, God bless her, has always wondered if I was gay. I don't blame her. I love to dress up, have an unmatchable knowledge of pop music, and hadn't yet married a woman to give her grandchildren (again, the end game). One day in the car, she finally caved.

"Sooo," she began. "Are there any girls you're interested in?"

"Yes, mother, there are a lot of girls I'm interested in." My sarcastic response, although completely true, only served to entertain me.

"You know what I mean." Of course I did. She was trying to have an open dialogue and I was not making it easy. The radio continued to fill the car ride around the lake in Kirkland, Washington, until she mustered up an attempt at pass number two. A smile cracked across her face as she perked up and popped her torso towards me, comfortably in the driver's seat of my brother's red Honda Accord.

"I have a question for you and don't get mad," she started, indicating that it would probably make me mad. The wonderful thing about my mom is that she repeated herself so often that I knew what she was going to say before she said it. That, coupled with the genetic connection, gave me a headstart on formulating my response.

"Yes mother, what is your question." I stated with an equal but opposite smirk sprouting across my face.

"Are you gay?" she giggled out. She would've been happy regardless of my response, and that's why I loved her.

"Yes, Mommy, I'm gay." Parenting is tough enough, and I wasn't making it any easier.

"No, I'm being serious. It's okay, you can can tell me."

I am, fortunately or unfortunately, not gay. Instead, I am stuck in the heterosexual world with all the changing traffic lights and potholes of the female gender.

———

The music played softly as we all arrived on site at their picturesque outdoor venue. The well-manicured lawn paved a long lane for each groomsman and bridesmaid to walk down. At the end of the grass runway, Diego waited for us to join at the gazebo. My brother, the ceremony officiant, stood next to him.

Everyone's head turned to the back, cueing me to start walking. After brief consideration, I tossed my tropical cane to the side and began waddling to the front. The beauty of being me is that no one knows when I'm joking or when I'm not. Friends and family, both new and old, laughed at what they believed was a bit. My tuxedo cover-up was doing a better job than we anticipated. I looked down to see my catheter pressing against my pants, which looked unmistakably like an erection. It's true; I was excited for Diego, but I wasn't that excited.

Despite the jeers and my geriatric pace, I eventually made it down the aisle. The rest of the party strutted their way up and James began. My brother worked with computers his whole life and somehow developed an incredible ability to speak about human connection along the way. My brother, a married man of two years, had everyone in tears.

Watching Diego get married gave the single groomsmen hope. Contrary to popular belief, being single at weddings sucks. Instead of reveling in personal love stories, we're all scavenging for someone or something to cling to. Love was in the air, and so was the inebriation of all the single people in attendance. With no drink to distract me, I focused on the best-man speech. This would be my second best-man speech, and I was afraid I wouldn't be able to express everything in my head. There are a lot more bad best-man and maid-of-honor speeches than there are good. Being succinct was key to success. The maid of honor usually recounted her childhood memories with the bride, while the best man traditionally roasted the groom. Also, why do we call them a groom? Regardless, I looked at this speech as my Oscar moment. I had won best man in a friendship that had seen ups and downs, hugs and fights, joy and utter darkness. Through it all, I somehow helped groom a man worthy enough for a woman. Wait, was that what the term groom referred to? As the time grew closer, I furiously scribbled my final notes on the wedding program. Speeches that were typed at home and read off a page were automatic bombs. The audience wanted to believe it was coming from the heart and reading off paper nullified that. My style is to write out the speech a day before, toss it, and then make a short outline at the beginning of the reception. The emotions of the day framed everything differently than being at home on the computer.

The maid of honor finished her speech, and I was waiting on the groom's side to take center stage. With tropical cane support, I arrived to find everyone's absolute attention fixated on me. I put the mic to my mouth and addressed the bride's family, all from the Midwest.

"Hello," I began, "my name is Ross and I am Diego's best friend. Welcome to this incredible wedding." Smiling, I waddled around like a penguin in a tuxedo to face Diego's family.

"Hola, me llamo Ross," rolling the R off my tongue extra hard. "Bienvenido a esta increíble boda." With one cultural joke in the can, I proceeded to praise and poke fun at someone who was truly a brother to me.

"Diego is a guy who always puts everyone first, and there's no one here that he hasn't stuck his neck out for, or been there for before we even asked. He's a guy who has taught me to go after what you want with absolute passion. I think we can all agree that he knew, and *we* knew, that you had found 'the one' when you met your now wife." Everyone smiled in agreement.

"The road to love is tough to navigate when you are as good looking as Diego. I'd like to take a moment to thank a couple people that helped him arrive at this amazing woman beside him. Thank you to Alexis, Katie, Shannon, Maria, Lindsey," I unfolded a small piece of paper into a full page and continued to list names, "Kimberly, Elle, Katie… did I already say Katie? Honestly, worth two mentions. Casey, Rachel, two Sarahs, definitely Kelly, and all of Diego's girlfriends whose names were either forgotten or never known in the first place. Thank you and rest in peace." This was funny because it was true. Diego and I had seen our fair share of women, but neither of us approached intimacy as a game. We had always been lovers. That doesn't sound right. We have always had a large capacity to love. While I tend to stay friends with my lovers, Diego kept them in the past. RIP ladies. Hope you enjoyed your curtain call.

The speech eventually ended with me crying because I'm an emotional person. The last time I gave a speech, I cried *uncontrollably*. The speech was for an award that my brother was receiving from the National Multiple Sclerosis Society. When I introduced him, I couldn't keep it together. I get particularly emotional when I talk about him because of how much he's meant to me in my life, and how much he's been there for me. Something clicked in my body and all composure went right out the window. It was no surprise that I had the same involuntary reaction with Diego.

"We've been through a lot together, both good and bad, and there's no one I feel better passing this cabrón off to. It is with absolute joy that I welcome you to the family, Grace. Diego, love you brother. Congratulations."

I raised my cane up, acknowledging their patience for my speech, and hobbled over to hug them. The night continued and I took a back seat to a majority of the usual drunken fun. Everyone was dancing but me, and it felt like a movie scene from a high school dance. There I was, reflecting upon my love life, my sex life, the lack of both, my family, and if I'd ever find a woman that would love me enough to clean the loaded bag of urine tied around my leg.

20

GIMME THE NEWS

I t wasn't long before I found myself back in the presence of Dr. Rajiv. This time for the second attempted catheter removal. Back where everybody knew my name, Dr. Rajiv's office had its usual senior suspects in the waiting room. I couldn't help but wonder if my future self was sitting across from me. I can't imagine what the three old men thought about me. With nothing else to do, I reached for a magazine. The only time I ever read print magazines were in waiting rooms. Southern Living seemed to always gravitate into my hands. It's just a well put together catalogue. I'm cool. I swear.

"Ross?" the nurse called.

"That's me!" Like a dart, I shot up and dropped my printed arrangement of picturesque gardens. This was the follow-up visit to get my catheter out, and like deja-vu, it was pretty much the same deal as the first time around. The OBGYN chair awaited my arrival while the big x-ray machine on the opposite wall continued to taunt me. Dr. Rajiv floated in with his billboard smile and immediately put me at ease.

He moved the catheter nozzle from my urine bag to the blue solution bag and filled me up. Like the previous visit, he needed me to feel uncontrollably full. Unlike the previous visit, I waited until I couldn't take anymore, twice over, before giving him the signal to remove the Foley. Once I gave the nod, Kate unsheathed the tube like Excalibur from the stone. My eyes popped wide open as my pain noise, which sounded like an elongated inhale on the word "oof," escaped. With a firm grip on the chair, I waited for the burning to pass as I slowly lay onto my side. Without knowing it, I had already started to pee.

———

The last time I peed uncontrollably was the Summer in between my junior and senior years of college. Diego and I lived in Los Angeles with four other people in a three bedroom apartment. One couple shared a room and I slept on the couch. I interned at Epic Records and the KROQ morning show, Kevin & Bean, while Diego took an intensive acting workshop. One of the weekends, we took the legendary four-hour drive to Las Vegas. Cruising in my silver Honda Accord, we prepared for a weekend of heavy drinking, looking at girls we'd be too nervous to talk to, and casual downtime with Diego's uncle Tio. Tio wasn't his name, it was just the Spanish word for uncle, which I didn't realize until my third semester in Spanish class. Tio was in town for a conference and let us stay in his hotel room for free -- keeping in line with the aforementioned first rule of doing Vegas. After seeing one of the 500 *Cirque du Soleil* shows in town, Diego and I departed from adult supervision.

We usually weren't the type to get ostentatious drinks that slung around our necks, but we did love fruity cocktails. He's Puerto Rican and I'm from Miami. It was natural. The problem with fruity cocktails in Vegas was that they were the novelty ones. So there we were, walking down the strip, each with a fishbowl full of alcohol. Worth noting, we already had one to wash down the oversized chicken and waffles from dinner. As that second bowl emptied, we scurried down the strip towards Omnia, the rooftop club at Caesar's Palace. The odds of us getting in were low, but what else were two guys that don't gamble to do in Vegas. And then, it happened. The tingle. The tingle shot through my bladder like a bullet with butterfly wings. Not only did I have to pee, I had to explode. My sensors were thrown off by the blinking lights, short skirts, and all the foreign men slapping stripper cards in my face. The stripper cards in Vegas were always something I forgot about as a staple in the city. This has to be the least effective direct-to-consumer marketing plan, but yet they've survived the test of time. Nevertheless, they have always surprised me.

"Yo Diego, I need to pee. Bad." He urged me to hold it as we picked up the pace. My intoxication levels were rising.

"Dude, you're fine." He apologized to the people around me as I swatted stripper cards and various Vegas riff raff that were between me and the next restroom. Wherever we were going, I wanted to get there faster. We cleared out of the brush and stepped onto a long, outdoor escalator. The action subsided.

"Yo, be cool," I said looking forward.

"What?" He was rightfully confused.

"I'm gonna go right now."

"What?" He said checking for people around. "Wait five more minutes." It was too late.

"Don't look at me," my guilty tone spoke plainly, "I'm already going." I had unzipped and untucked on the escalator for a full bathroom break.

"You're an idiot." As the escalator neared the top, Diego casually looked off into the distance while I pretended to be on my cell phone. Fake phone calls were my go-to move for public urination. I sympathize with women who have to pee in public. They couldn't pop a squat and pretend to be on their cell phone. Reception was not better closer to the ground. As the escalator neared the top, I shook the lingering drips out and tucked the floppy disk back in the drive. Sometimes, you've just gotta go.

———

"Ross, let's try and get it on the pad," Dr. Rajiv requested. Rolling over a little more, I tried to control myself with minimal success. I was spurting out pee and hoping Dr. Rajiv could time his photography well. After a couple rounds, I comfortably waded in a warm baby pool of my own urine. The doctor nodded to signal that he had what he needed. Kate handed me a towel as he reviewed the images. He mumbled "good" a couple of times and the relief in my bladder carried through the rest of my body. Unlike the dramatics of my previous office visit, I had completely healed up with no leakage. He took one last grip on my member and examined the stitches. They had slowly been dissolving. I've never been more diligent in cleaning a wound than I had been with the Frankenstein stitches that went around my shaft. Three times a day, I carefully swabbed my penis with cleaning solution and a topical ointment. The stitches looked like a bad barbed wire tattoo. I don't think there's such a thing as a good barbed wire tattoo, but that's what it looked like.

With my reinforced urethra ready for action, the doctor had me take the show into an actual bathroom. He needed to test my urine volume and overall strength of stream. Strength of stream, despite how it sounded, was not an Olympic judging criteria. It was the velocity at which I was peeing. It's amazing that I had been peeing my whole life without knowing the technicalities of this feat. I shuffled down the hall, still unfamiliar with walking untubed, to a small toilet with various meters around it. If I thought peeing in row of urinals at a football game was tough, this brought in a whole new level of intimidation.

"Good luck," Kate said as she hit a button next to the toilet machine and closed the door. A buzz from one of the machines hit my ears. The last time I heard a noise like that was when I was 12, which also happened to be the year I stopped peeing the bed in my sleep. Most "normal" kids don't pee the bed that late in life, but clearly my issues had history. My parents, God bless them, tried many methods to potty train me, but only one gadget did the trick. They put me in underwear, lined with electric wires connected to an external battery pack, that would shock me awake if they got wet. The battery pack was a small, black rectangular box and the wires were red. I didn't really think of how fucked up that was, on behalf of both my parents (they tried) and the product's inventor, until now. That being said, it worked.

As the stream machine buzzed through the tiny bathroom, I took a moment to literally and figuratively reflect in the mirror. This was the moment I had been working towards for the past month. A month ago, the ability to pee on my own stopped being a right and started being a gift. I turned to face the toilet and pulled my pants down. Staring at the toilet, my internal control center began sending signals. I knew that my bladder was full, but the rusted buttons still needed pushing. Like a magician, I commanded my bladder to go.

HUZZAH!

Nothing. I flopped my dongle around as a physical reminder of its duty to the body. Even though I had just let the coffee drip for the photography session, I felt plenty more in the pot. The longer I stood there, the more daunting it became. I could feel a slight throb in my knees, and my throat had gone dry. My body started to quiver. The narration at the end of Michael Jackson's "Thriller" would have been an appropriate voice over.

And then, it happened. The tingle. An eruption from the soles of my feet shot up my legs and hit my core like a bus. My balls quivered and, for a second, I thought I was about to orgasm. Instead, I began peeing like a defunct sprinkler. What the fuck was my body doing? It sounded like cups of water were being dumped into the toilet. When the body doesn't function the way it's supposed to, it sure is embarrassing. Luckily no one was around to see the rodeo. As I wrangled the horse into the stable, the stream meter, stationed next to the toilet, started printing results. A line graph recorded a continuous account of my escapade. I started to lean closer to the machine, but quickly realigned after missing the toilet. Peeing into the robot toilet was my first mission. Despite having minor anxiety that something would be off, I was peeing on my own. With audible laughter, I signified another milestone of recovery. I couldn't believe this moment had arrived. It was the little things in life.

The doctor scanned the results and we shared in our success together. I wanted to hug him, but we had already been intimate enough for a lifetime. With a strong handshake, Dr. Rajiv sent me off.

"So doc, one month..." I started to say as a reminder more to myself.

"Exercises for one month without stress," he said.

"And no sex for another two," I continued.

"That's right, and you're going to be very careful."

Damn skippy I was going to be careful. Sex felt so far away, but it's always worth a reminder. As I stepped out of the office, catheter free, I raised my arms up to the sun and took in all of its energy. I was free. At long last, I was free.

21

SENSE MEMORY

I was free. I was alone, sitting at home with a lot to grapple with. Life is full of comedy and drama, each willing to swap places on a moment's notice. Parker hadn't been absent from my mind as much as she was from my dialogue. Back at home, I sat on my bed, took off my shoes, and placed them next to a pair of boots she'd bought me. My closet has always consisted of clothes I had been gifted, handed down, or acquired after a film shoot. Parker bought me these boots for no occasion. She was simply being her thoughtful, generous self. I graciously accepted them, but in a moment of reflection, knew it had no bearing on my attraction to her. There was a reason I knew that marrying for money wasn't an option, and it wasn't my teenage dowry. I had been with someone that inundated me with gifts before, and it was in a much darker chapter, one that I didn't choose to put in my narrative.

Towards the end of my college career, I had been hooking up with a girl a year older and much wealthier than me. We had met in class and she offered to help shoot promotional photos for a benefit improv show. The show I was putting up, called Toys for Laughs, doubled as a toy drive during the holidays. The extension of her wealth in support of my career led to a physical relationship.

She gifted me electronics and bought me meals all in between getting laid. It would be hard for anyone to jump ship without incredible foresight, let alone a poor college student in the arts who'd recently lost his virginity.

When I left abroad for my final semester, which was made possible because of a scholarship, I said it was best we end our intimacy. Although she did not take this well, she reiterated that she thought I was incredibly talented and wanted to help me however she could. I promised to stay in touch.

Halfway through our semester, she contacted me about shooting and writing for a well-known travel publication that she freelanced for. She could pay me, but she would also have to join me. She was exploiting me, but I didn't know that. I, unable to work or make money abroad, thought this was a way to make money and get experience in my field. She sent me a camera to play with the week before she arrived, and we would soon be shooting in various locations together.

Physically and emotionally, I had moved on. I let it be known that we were not going to be romantic, and she told me that was understood. I was interested in another classmate, whom I had spent a considerable amount of time with in Spain, where we were studying.

When she arrived, she had a bunch of presents to remind me of home. She had even bought me an iPod (which was not something everyone owned back then), loaded with music she had bought for me. It didn't take long for her to revert back to old habits. Soon after the presents were open, she started kissing me. It's important that I mention our attraction didn't wane, and my body was ready to jump right back in. In our Sevillano hotel, I had to quickly end this, reminding her that I was romantically spending time with someone else. After hours of talking, I reminded her of our understanding. Admittedly, this was all a terrible idea from the start, but hindsight is 20/20. A couple days later, we were on assignment with a group tour in the south of Ireland.

The tour company booked separate rooms for everyone, but

she had made sure we were staying in the same room. Although I remember being incredibly uneasy about this, I thought the inconvenience of making it an issue outweighed any potential problems. After our first day of touring, we were dropping our gear in the room to join everyone at the bar. She gave me a shot glass she'd bought from a souvenir store that said "Kiss Me, I'm Irish." I rolled my eyes as much then as I do now at the thought of anyone genuinely buying something that cheesy. Not soon after, she asked if I was still attracted to her. I answered honestly (because I'm a moron), and said I was, but that that didn't change anything. Another two hours of fighting ensued, she said she could take a helicopter and just leave. That sounded ridiculous, but I believed her. She had, after all, built herself up as having an incredibly wealthy and connected family. As someone who hates to argue, I found a temporary end to the conversation and left the hotel to join everyone else at the tiny, local bar.

I was two pints of Guinness in when she showed up with a stern look across her face. After another hour of avoiding each other, she brought me a drink.

"I'm still very attracted to you," she said, "and I don't know why you would've come on this trip if you weren't still attracted to me too." She was right. I shouldn't have been there, but I was. Blame the lure of money and sex, or our inability to see clearly in obvious situations. She didn't apologize before our brief conversation ended, and I went back with my pint to another table. Some time after, I blacked out.

I came back to my senses on our hotel bed, unable to move. The only light in the room came through a tiny window that was held together by a wooden frame far older than me. Although I stared out the window, the light that punctured through it wasn't the reason I woke up. My pants were being pulled off. She was saying something, but I don't remember what. My next memory of this surreal scene was her grinding on top of me and the noise of the stale bed frame hitting the wall.

Thought isn't really consistent in moments like these. I

remember thinking that we were going to wake everyone up, and that we were supposed to be the media professionals on the trip. She grinded on me and whispered continuously, as though to guide me through the haze. Seeing the bedpost hit the wall felt like I was watching a loop of an old blue-tinted film. The pervasive sound of hollow wood reverberated through the room. In that moment, it was the only thing I sought to stop. It was the only thing I thought I could stop. With all the strength I could muster, I flung my right arm onto the frame and gripped its faded finish. Though I tried to mutter dissent, the focus was on pulling the frame in enough to keep it from making more noise. But I couldn't. My body had failed, and I had little choice. I observed her silhouette as it pressed into me with devilish intent until the flicker finally faded.

———

Parker's kindness had an unintentional effect. A pair of boots sparked this reminder of why I am the way I am, at least partially. Who we are is not always a reflection of who we necessarily want to be. Sometimes, it's a product of who we've been forced to become. We harbor these memories triggered by touch, taste, scent, sound, and sight. They live, wanted and unwanted, in desolate parts of our subconscious. I forgot that she was a chapter in my story. Even though its subject matter doesn't match the overall tone, leaving it out would have been unfitting. What we've been through shapes how we get through what we go through, and I had been through much worse than this freak accident. That's probably why I could laugh about it, and it's definitely why I could appreciate women like Parker. I was lucky. I could think of Parker without confusing where my attraction was coming from. Only once we've felt trapped can we fully understand the feeling of being free.

22

TINY DANCER

I was free, but the road to recovery was long and hard. My marching orders were no foul play and no foreplay. Instead, I had to go through "exercises without stress" two times a day, every day. That meant get an erection and do nothing with it for fifteen minutes. I used to just call that middle school. HEYO! But seriously, the penis was a muscle and it needed stretching and strengthening like anywhere else. This exercise quickly became the highest form of restraint in modern day love.

Luckily, I have been exercising self control my whole life. I'm a dog, and dogs just want to eat (even when they're not hungry). The greatest test a straight man faces in a democratic nation was to keep eye contact with woman who has cleavage on display. I'm not even talking about a lot of cleavage. Men would just as quickly look at a chest without any bust if it was exposed. The science behind this has never made sense. I don't have an answer to this phenomenon. Men's eyes are attracted to curves and women's eyes are attracted to lines. I have no problem with a woman who has a strong jawline, but it doesn't have the same magical effect as a woman's chest. The weird part is that a fully exposed breast isn't the tractor beam, it's just The Cleavage (royalty deserves capital letters).

Even though looking at The Cleavage came with little perverse intent, men have to exercise self control to keep their eyes up. If casual cleavage exposure was the normal test of a man's control, push-up bras were the LSATs. Like yoga pants to the booty, push-up bras have created illusions of grandeur since their inception in 1964. For the record, I don't advocate for these. Magic tricks are cool, but being unequivocally yourself has always been sexier. But again, I'm just a dog and I will want to look regardless. I can't help it. I'm wired this way. When people say that guys think about sex every six seconds, I've already thought "sex seconds?" It's not fun. Robin Williams said that men have a brain and a penis, and God only gave us enough blood to run one at a time. Here's the hard part, masturbation has always been my coping mechanism for a filthy mind. When an erection got in the way of a productive day, I'd just rub one out of my body and, thus, out of my mind. Once the moose had been juiced, I could go back to living my life in peace. Does it make sense? Absolutely!

Does that mean that I just Michael Jackson *Beat It* with every pop star? Absolutely not. As a guy, I have to beware of bullets in the chamber. We can only reload so many times in a day, which is to say that our semen count isn't infinite. Women have this amazing superpower that allows them to have multiple orgasms in a row. Are you serious? I can't even find the G spot, let alone the button that triggers multiple orgasms. Meanwhile, guys make life-or-death decisions about when to put on the squeeze. When to choke the chicken. Duke the bishop. Flog the dog. Beat the boxer. Crank. Churn the butter. Have a Roy. Have a Sherman. Play some pocket pool. Or just engage in really safe sex (no partners allowed). In any case, if I thought there'd be a chance of intercourse in the ensuing twelve hours, I exercised self control like a diabetic in a candy store. Often times, I'd have internal debates mid-stroke on whether or not to finish. If the jury decided there's a chance of getting laid, I immediately stopped the car and got out.

My friend Jonah always impressed me with his self-restraint habits. He employed a method he called "harvesting." Harvesting referred to the period of time that he would give himself to replenish his sperm bank. Harvesting meant no masturbating. No pole vaulting, pumping, or popping the top. Jonah claimed to harvest every Thursday, Friday, and Saturday. Although impossible to prove, I was impressed. Regardless of crop, we both acknowledged the correlation between sex drive and how long it's been since waxing the dolphin.

So there I was, staring at my woody while watching a full scene of porn. I'd never felt more like a benchwarmer than when watching porn and doing nothing but paying attention to the production itself. I wonder if the dialogue was scripted or improvised, and which would be more impressive on the actors' part. Also, do I call them actors or performers? It's impossible not to offend someone with everything we say, but I tried. This dilemma has never been more clear than it has been with strippers, which I found out in Portland when I unknowingly went on a date with one.

"Jazz? Tap?" I guessed, after she told me she worked as dancer.

"Close," she played.

"Ballet? Swing? What are we talking here?" I continued.

"Exotic," she responded matter-of-factly. We were two stiff drinks in and my brain didn't calculate what to say next correctly.

"Oh... like an exotic stripper?" I said across the table in broad daylight.

"Exotic *dancer*," she snapped back. I have never called a stripper a stripper to her face ever since.

———

"We're going to need at least four cases," the porn actor said into his phone. I couldn't remember the last time I watched the scene work on an adult site. The guy just so happened to walk by a pool where a couple of women in American flag bikinis were harassing him about going to a party.

"Hi girls." He continued to the non-existent person on the phone, "I'm going to need to call you back."

The video I was watching had over nine *million* views. The three pornstars in this video, Jessica Jaymes, Nicole Aniston, and Lisa Ann, have links to their individual biography pages in the caption. On their bio pages were the total number of video views they each had, and the three of them totaled for over one *billion* views. Of course I had time to look at their individual statistics pages and do the math. The Pornhub website, which housed the video, was actually really well built and easy to navigate. With low barriers to entry and a high active user base, the porn industry was a prime test ground for UI/UX testing before it hits mainstream. Guess where the original video thumbnail preview came from? It wasn't YouTube. After all that quality time, I decided to side with "performers." I never really believed them when they "didn't order a pizza" or their "husband wasn't home."

I spent more time looking at my erect penis than I ever thought I would. A month after the break, it looked more like an experiment than a weapon of mass destruction. The stitches hadn't dissolved as much as I thought they would. They stuck out, ready to catch a fiber from a blanket or my underwear, sending a sting through my body. Dicks weren't pretty to begin with, and this didn't help. I had this half salami that had been to the butcher and back. It might have been all the porn I was watching, but post-sex guilt hung heavy. The more I looked down, the more I felt down. I know it sounds dumb, but that was my reality. I was alone with my untouchable, throbbing whistle. Moving the joystick around, I knew the stitches holding the beast together would dissolve, but the scar would stay. My broken banana was a symbol for where my life was. My frankencock was alive, but I knew he would never be the same. First world problems with a capital D.

"Come on," the porn performer pleaded towards the end of her scene, "I need your cum." First of all, do you ever really *need* his swimmers? That's a lot of pressure to put on a guy even if he was getting paid. And do male performers get paid? I hope so, because they must work under a lot of pressure. In any case, the twenty minute routine came to an end and I was exhausted. Physical therapy never had such highs and lows.

23

RAISE A GLASS TO FREEDOM

I hadn't gone out since the accident and what better way to revive my social life than on Halloween. Halloween is everyone's excuse to dress up in an outfit that either shows off their body or shows off their wit. Most normal people use this night as a chance to be more silly than usual, but dressing up is more than an annual occasion for me. At a young age, it started as a profession and turned into everyday life. Dressing up began when I was a mere four years old. I was a kid model in Miami for the then-small (now huge) agency, Irene Marie on South Beach. Basically, I peaked early. Anyone who has ever modeled or pretended to be a model on the internet knows the necessity of multiple outfits. The first time I remember dressing up was for my composite card, which was an oversized business card with pictures and measurements. A comp card was basically the physical version of a dating app profile for casting directors to comb through. After being signed, the talent shoots the photos for these comp cards on the advice of their agent.

"We're going to want three to five looks. One close up of just the face, smiling. Big smile too. Not necessarily a smile with those teeth, which look like they're falling out," the agent advised, giggling disingenuously. "Smile with those big blue eyes. Then a full body shot in a fun pose. We want to show off your personality, so it's important to really have fun with it -- Mom, you can help with that one. Trust me, they can tell." She continued while we sat cluelessly in an office where the walls were plastered with pictures of beautiful people. "Ross, what's your favorite sport?"

"Um, I play basebawl and I like basketbawl," I said in my adolescent voice.

"Lots of baseball players. Mom, maybe have him sit on a basketball. Sports are always good. Backwards hat, have him run around and build up a sweat." This continued until my mom had enough notes to take my pictures. Oh yeah, my mom took my pictures because we never paid someone to do something we could do ourselves for less. For better or worse, it worked. I continued playing dress up in catalogues for stores like JCPenney and magazines like *Parents Magazine*. This was the stage of my life that I define as poisoning the well. Back then, kids weren't constantly in front of a camera. I got the taste early, and it never left. While most kids went on to study business, science, and finance, I sat in the classroom reading scripts and practicing my English accent for the upcoming Agatha Christie play. Even though I got to play different characters on stage, dressing up on October 31st held a special place in my heart.

I dressed up for every Halloween I can remember, and I can remember every costume I ever had. That's because every year I wore one of three costumes from age 5 to 15 that my mother, God bless her, would choose. None of these costumes were bought and none of them were made. They were all repurposed parts of my regular life. The first and most obvious was a baseball player. My parents paid good money so that I could participate in Little League. Bat, gloves, uniform, hat, shoes, and socks were all ready to go. My mom would prep me like getting candy was the same as playing in an actual game. With my bat over one shoulder, I'd stick out my glove (which was on, of course) and wait for a candy deposit.

"And what are you?" Adults were really good at making kids feel good. The fact that people would still ask me was, in retrospect, ridiculous.

"I'm a basebawl player!" I'd respond with the enthusiasm of someone who believed they could actually be a professional baseball player. After four years of that costume, it was time for a change. The next extracurricular activity that required purchasing a uniform was Tae Kwon Do. Long before Mixed Martial Arts and all of the subsequent forms of self defense, Tae Kwon Do ruled the land as the karate of choice for white people. Although more expensive than baseball, karate taught discipline and respect, both of which every parent wanted their kid to have more of at that age. In addition to paying for classes, my parents had to buy me a gi, the all white Japanese outfit that can be best described as a stiff robe. The gi cost $30. For someone who strictly wore hand-me-downs and clearance items, I understood why it needed more use at that price.

"For Halloween this year," my mom deliberated, "you're going to be in karate." This took a moment to understand. I wasn't going to be the Karate Kid. I wasn't going to be a ninja turtle. I was simply going to be "in karate." By the time Halloween rolled around, I had only moved up one level from beginner, which was from a white belt to a yellow belt. This wasn't exactly impressive. To compensate, I dug through my dad's closet and found a brown leather belt to put on. Brown belts are one level below black belts, which are worn in the highest level of Tae Kwon Do. Needless to say, my mind took creative liberties from an early age. When I'd ring on doorbells, instead of sticking out my glove, I'd demonstrate a wide arrange of blocks. High block, low block, inside block, outside block… that was all I'd been taught. After receiving candy, I'd bow and say thank you. We can honestly get away with so much stupid shit as kids. The next time I have sex (Summer 2048), I'm going to bow and say thank you. After two years of being "in karate" for Halloween, I actually stopped doing karate. I had also stopped playing baseball. My mom, a history major, had to dig deep to come up with a new costume for me. After digging around the house for something new, she decided to go with what she knew.

"For Halloween this year" my mom deliberated, "Why don't you just dress as a woman?" That's right. My mom handed me a pile of her clothes and told me, a chubby middle schooler, to crossdress. I thought this was hilarious. Normal boys probably would have put up more resistance, but we waved bye bye to normal when I signed up for circus class as an extracurricular activity during the summer before fifth grade. I wore a blonde wig, a black bra under an open denim shirt, and jeans with Converse sneakers. I stuffed the bra with two stuffed animals, a bear and a moose. To make matters better or worse (unclear), I went trick or treating with my friend Dave, who my mom also dressed as a woman. When we'd say "Trick or Treat" at each house, the owners didn't bother asking what we were. Had I known the urban definition of a trick back then, this would have been way better. If anyone gave us good candy, we'd offer to give them a performance. Instead of a striptease, we sang the N*Sync song "Tearin Up My Heart" and did a dance together. Years later, Dave and I were in an emo pop punk band harvesting our teen angst together.

The next year for Halloween, I dressed as a woman again but to my friend Brooke's house party. The mother of that house took creative liberties with my costume. She gave me balloons to replace the stuffed animals in my bra and glow in the dark pasties, which was when I learned what pasties were.

"Don't tell your mom I did this," Brooke's mom whispered. To this day, I wonder if she thought my mom was suppressing my sexuality and that had I changed right after getting dropped off, or if she didn't want my mom to feel like she one-upped her work.

The truth was that my mom, like every mom, wanted a girl. When she got me, I filled the gap of what a daughter would've done. One of the joys a mother and daughter have together is shopping. In my trove of odd talents, I am a phenomenal guy to shop for clothes with. My mom would take me to either Marshall's, T.J. Maxx, or Ross, and sit me down outside the dressing room. She would come out and model whatever discount top she had chosen, and I hit her with the truth like time was running out. Whether it didn't fit, the color wasn't right, or the cut was too low, I wasted no time and always trusted my gut. Point being, I make a great mean girl.

I should mention there was one exception. The first year my brother and I went trick or treating together was the one year that my brother and I both had original costumes. I, holding a realistic Colt .45, was dressed as a cowboy, and my brother (I can't even believe this is true) was dressed as Saddam Hussein.

———

Fast forward to current day Halloween. Two holidays I don't love in New York City were Halloween and New Year's Eve. The city doesn't need an excuse to have drunk people in masks running around, and there were never any cabs on New Years. As a last minute costume, I grabbed the puppet of myself that I own (doesn't everybody?) and dressed as the puppet. Essentially, I dressed as myself. I headed with my friend Dan, who dominated the costume game as a Daft Punk DJ, to a bar in the Lower East Side that some friends had rented out. More importantly, I knew Parker would be there. Parker and I had been texting on and off, and I wanted to see her. In the end, we're all suckers for pain and gluttons for drama.

Parker spotted me from across the room and gave me the "hi" look. When two people with history were at a bar, it nullified everyone else in that bar. Regardless of all the people there that I hadn't seen, we magnetized towards each other. Parker, despite not being a big costume person, dressed up as a flapper girl. I hated the word flapper, but the look was a good mix of classy and sexy. Flappers (ugh) were the kind of sexy other girls wouldn't talk shit about from across the room either.

"Hi," she melodically said to me in a muted tone.

"Ello," I said in my overdone English accent. We talked and used alcohol to navigate through the choices of how to act with each other. We'd subtly tug on each other's clothes to indicate our undefined physical boundaries. Like a lot of bar interactions, ours meant little. I dialed back my drinking when it was clear that she had dialed up hers. People have the tendency to get really drunk in emotionally confusing situations. I've never been the "I'm just going to get really drunk if she's there" type, but I have been the "wear my mom's clothes" type so who am I to judge? My high school girlfriend got really drunk at my senior prom (remember I wasn't drinking back then) because she didn't want to think about me leaving her for college. My college girlfriend got really drunk one night and called me crying because she thought I was going to leave her like the main character does to his girlfriend in the teen sensation book *Twilight*. Oddly enough, the main character of *Twilight* was a vampire and, in the end, I did leave her.

"Ross," she whispered, "I'm ready to go home." If she was ready, I was ready. Why would I want to stay out if she wanted to be in my bed? Logistics have always been a pain point of mine. I always chose logic over expectation. When it came to getting home, we had the choice of walking or riding. Sometimes the quickest option wasn't the best. If we took a taxi, we'd be there so quick that her head would be spinning too hard the second we hit the bed. According to me, she needed to lower the chances of vomiting and walk it off. If we walked though, would that make me look cheap? A guy never wants to look cheap. The bigger issue was that whatever decision I made didn't turn into one of those future talking points either. This could be a tack on my personality that she'd let sit under the surface for months. Then, one day we'd be finished with some friends at a bar and I'd suggest walking home. After all of that germinating, she'd look at me, note her heels, and say something like "this isn't Halloween." Pages of internal dialogue flew through my head, but logic won and we took a hike.

"Hang in there," I said. We walked up Allen Street and onto 1st Ave. Like a newborn giraffe, Parker wobbled her way back to my place using me as a leaning board the whole way. The problem with being a flapper girl was that that costume went from sexy to raggedy real quick. Her makeup had smeared and there wasn't a damn thing to do but own the looks I was getting. It was in this rare moment that I wished she had chosen to be what every girl chose to be for at least one Halloween, a cat. The only makeup to smear on a cat was its whiskers, and then you look like a chimney sweep. And who doesn't love a good chimney sweep?

When we arrived at my apartment, I guided her up the stairs and sat her down on the sofa. It was like she couldn't keep her head upright on her neck.

"Come sit over here next to me. I'm not a vampire, I don't bite," she said without knowing the history of my vampire association. Before I knew it, we had kissed. Then, we made out like middle schoolers that hadn't quite figured out what to do with our tongues. It had been two months since I kissed her, and it felt really nice. Then the progression began. The next step on the road to sex was one person's hand touching the other person's special place. Her delicate hand slid down into the danger zone, and I did what the woman traditionally has the choice of doing -- I gently brushed her away.

"Whoa easy killer," I reminded her, "Elevator is still not in service." She stopped and gazed at me through her glassy blue eyes. As with most late night moments of romance, it ended with one of us falling asleep. After college, I self imposed a rule in relationships whereby no serious talks take place after 11:30pm. I imposed this rule after multiple instances of falling asleep during otherwise serious conversations with girlfriends. We would usually be laying in bed, and that's traditionally where sleep happened. Needless to say, Parker zonked out on my chest mid-conversation.

When I woke up the following morning, Parker's head lay on my arm. Guys all over the world are used to this. We accepted the loss of one arm when laying in bed with a partner. One of my pet peeves was waking people up, so the guilt also stopped me from retaking any limbs lost in the cuddling process.

"Parker?" she slouched into my room and held the doorway to steady herself. Her hair was all over her face and her eyes were puffy. "Wow, um...did I...did *we*?"

I shook my head. Parker sighed and closed her eyes. "Yeah, I'm sorry, I don't really remember much of what happened."

"That's ok," I laughed. "You were really drunk, and really cute. And you really wanted to do more things."

"Yeah?" she laughed, acknowledging that I was also subtly patting myself on the back, "Did we make out?"

"That we did," I said. She smiled and I returned it. "Since we're not having sex, should we just eat all day and be lazy?"

Food was the next best thing to sex and sometimes can even be better, depending on the dish and the sex. We spent the rest of the evening just hanging out on the sofa, talking about everything from my best friend's wedding to the weird x-ray test. We even talked about that uncomfortable time I asked her to be my girlfriend, which seemed like forever ago.

"I still can't believe you did that," Parker said.

"Yeah, me either." Then the elongated pause. "I still really like you."

"I like you too. You know that." This was how the idea of an "us" continued. It's so hard to end what was already over. Blame it on globalization, but goodbyes don't really exist anymore. With our social media lives making us so accessible, we never have to bid farewell. We used to say "be right back." That doesn't exist anymore, we're always there.

"So, no sex?" she asked. I was experiencing true gender role reversal. This was the third time saying no to sexual activity in 24 hours. So there we were, two people who clearly liked each other, in this relationship that we were figuring out, reading one another like an open book, and having absolutely no sex. Is this what marriage was like? Honesty and no sex?

The conversation evolved back into The Talk terrority, and we were at a standstill. Was the shadow of what we'd been through too dark for us to move on? It was a whole new level of complicated. Parker and I agreed on most things, but we also didn't see a way to keep it going. Should we just agree never to see each other again? Should we keep seeing each other, just making out like a couple of teenagers and leave it at that? What about when I could actually have sex again, would that change things? Would her career still be a priority? Dating an entrepreneur had its challenges. The truth of the matter was that having a relationship took time, effort, attention, and work just like a start-up. People weren't accustomed to walking away from a situation that bonded them so strongly together because of logic. Parker and I hadn't reached a solution yet. I liked her. She liked me. We couldn't have sex. That's where we left it after being delivered three meals, two of which were Thai. Also, why is Thai food so delicious? And do Thai restaurant owners roll their eyes every time someone orders Pad Thai? And did I get Thai street cred if I ordered something that wasn't Pad Thai? If so, did ordering Pad See Ew qualify? Finally, have I been capitalizing the name of dishes because they were so delicious?

Parker left my apartment that evening with a lot more questions than answers, but neither of us were giving up the feelings we had for each other.

24

TAKE YOUR PANTS OFF AND JACKET

"I'm sick of this shit," I said to myself wandering the hospital halls, and I was. It was a lot easier to be positive around other people than when I was alone. Being negative was easy because the best things in life are rare (hot tubs, airplanes without screaming children, steaks). I've silently fought this balance throughout my life. Going to the doctor alone created a particular breed of morbid thoughts. The checkup with my primary surgeon, Dr. Herm, started soon and I barely made it through the door on time. Everyone knows that appointment times meant nothing at the doctor, but it still gave me anxiety. The man at the front desk identified me and smiled. My mood immediately transformed into his.

"Hey Ross, good to see you!" I had no clue who he was, but we exchanged smiles. Carl, as he told me, stood in the original x-ray room where Dr. Wang put a camera in my disco stick for an eternity. They clearly ran a family business in the urology department. The primary surgeon, Dr. Herm, popped out to shake my hand. I hadn't seen him since I laid on the gurney in the operating room.

"Hi Ross, it's great to see you. I just got off the phone with Dr.

Rajiv," he continued with positive reinforcement, "Everything sounds great. Your healing looks great and you're already getting erections?" They had normalized this kind of talk for me. It was like Dr. Rajiv and Dr. Herm were my two recently divorced, gay dads guiding me through puberty. We walked through my urine diary, a self explanatory log of my streams, and eventually got to the hands-on portion of the day. Pulling my pants down in front of grown men had become a regular feature over the last month. Dr. Herm put on his blue latex gloves, which forever reminded me of the Blink 182 album cover for *Enema of the State*, and took a pistol grip. The doctor intimately examined my penis. As he delicately held my little soldier, I launched a barrage of questions.

Why was my scar circular? In my head, the doctor would cut down the shaft and open it up like a kielbasa. In reality, he did a radial incision and peeled skin up and down like automatic doors. Half gross, half awesome. Full on Frankencock.

What are these two bumps in the middle of my penis? This question would have a different answer if the bumps were topical, but mine were under the skin. This was where he stitched up the tear on my muscle tissues (the corpus cavernosum). The scar tissue that formed over it created these weird bulb-like bumps. My new tagline might have to be "bulbed for her pleasure."

Why does it hurt when I'm hard? I was experiencing pain when I was erect, and not the usual emotional pain. There was an actual dip in the middle of my jimmy where my urethra was. The pain came from stretching the tissue, which had shortened in its repair. This extremely minor amount of lost tissue also caused my curvature to change. My penis now pointed straight, instead of its usual slightly upward lift. Not many men can say they have lived with two penises. I wasn't convinced this new edition was going to be better than the vintage coin either.

He walked me through the rest of my schwartz issues, reinforcing care and carefulness. The Frankenstein scar, the scar tissue, the stitches, and the whole event made much more sense now. As he flopped the mini-me around, I imagined he was also judging his body of work. This was, after all, a piece of art. I wouldn't say the Mona Lisa, but we were both satisfied with the final product. After the gloves came off, he handed me samples of an erection enhancement drug. There's no way to play it cool when that that part of life arrives. Instead of saying I didn't need it, I stashed as much as he'd give me while pondering the superpowers of a Performance Enhancing Drug penis (PED PEN).

"When am I cleared to start using this thing?" I asked, still trying to play it cool.

"You can most certainly work with yourself carefully," he said as I decoded his professional way of saying have a tug, "and you can start having *very* gentle intercourse in another month." Dr. Herm spoke with the ghosts of past patients that didn't heed his advice. I did a rough calculation. Sex time landed in mid December, right around my birthday.

"I hate to ask this, but what are the odds of this happening again," I knew the answer, but needed to hear it.

"Like any injury," he lectured, "you're operating at an increased risk of it happening again. If a football player tears an ACL, he's at a disadvantage. Any break or tear never goes back to one hundred percent. Your body is healing very well, but you still need to be *very* careful moving forward. Any traumatic injury takes six months to heal as much as it will. So just be very careful." He had to have been laughing a little on the inside.

"Doc," I vowed with a gigantic smile, "I will be making only the sweetest and gentlest of love from now on." We both knew that wouldn't be completely true, but at least I verbalized it. With that, I walked out of the room with a head full of existential thoughts and a bag full of penis pills. I paused at the top of the corridor and curiosity gripped me. I wanted to get a copy of my medical records while I was at the hospital.

Medical records were not easy to find. For whatever reason, I believed that all the hospitals I've ever been to store my medical history on the same, easily accessible medical cloud. In reality, none of them were connected nor were they even digital. After asking the officer at the information desk, I headed out to find the records room. Hospitals were twisted labyrinths where one wrong turn could net me radiation poisoning or a newborn baby. The medical records room, as it turned out, was actually a closet in the basement. As I creaked open the door, my eyes didn't believe what they saw.

"Hello," a beautiful looking woman said, "How can I help you?" I smiled back and played through a trapped-in-the-closet fantasy. Nothing says game like flirting over unflattering medical history. The poor woman working in the closet must have been an intern. No windows, fluorescent lights, and hospital air couldn't be a job someone interviewed for. I quickly realized that the medical records office was the hospital's equivalent to the DMV. A couple clipboards of paperwork, photo identification copies, and digital forms later, my request processed.

The records confirmed a lot of the details that I had anticipated. Some of them were even a lot more accurate than I had figured. Remember Carl and Dr. Wang with the black snake camera? I was pretty close about how long it took them to poke around. Dr. Wang told me sixty seconds, but it was two minutes and thirty seconds. I was relieved to know that I wasn't making everything up. Worth noting this random factoid; our memories are just a memory of us remembering our most recent memory. So the longer we try to remember something, the more faded it gets.

I left the hospital and, with it, the memories I'd made there. Love was waiting to be made, and I was ready to make it very, *very* gently. Before doing it with a partner, I needed to take a couple test shots on my own (per doctor's orders). I'd never gone this long without flapping my wings since I was a kid. In short, Christmas had arrived.

25

THE FIRST TIME

Does anyone remember the first time they masturbated? Everyone remembered when they lost their virginity, for better or worse, but that first orgasm was a little more elusive. The first time for me was hard to pinpoint. I did remember a lot of dry humping a particularly soft bedside pillow. This miniature pillow found its way between the bed and me and, as I rolled around one night, must've been in just the right spot. My little pillow became my little secret. I'd fold it in half to make a well cushioned vagina and go to town. Sometimes I would stand and bone it, and sometimes I'd lay down and let the pillow do the work. Love is love is love. My pillow got it either missionary or cowgirl and, after I finished, went right back in the closet. Later in life, this might be something to unpack with a therapist. I never used a sock. I didn't even use lotion. The touch, the feel of cotton was enough for me.

Back at home, the perfect evening unfolded for a picturesque launch. I was alone. The sun set behind the curtains, and I lit a couple of candles. Not. All that mattered was that no one was home, which meant I could keep the volume on. After all those hours of watching entire scenes, I suppose I had grown a fondness for them. I flicked on my computer and went straight to Pornhub in a private browser, of course. Gone were the days of clearing browser history. Gone were the days of downloading videos to the hard drive and putting them in folders labeled "English." Gone were the days of slow internet connections where it took three minutes to download a nudie picture. The days of free streaming HD video had arrived and all the deviant have since rejoiced.

"It is time," I said in my familiar Rafiki impersonation.

I went straight for the high production value porn with top shelf porn stars. I could never be bothered by all the fetish categories, which was surprising given my theatrical background. With the computer fan roaring, I opened six windows with different videos in each. Resized in a three-by-three arrangement on the screen, I paused to recognize the overkill I'd created, but this was America. I didn't want to watch one at a time. I didn't want to choose. I wanted it all, and I wanted it now. "Performers" with a diverse range of hair colors, various measurements, number combinations, and even a comic book parody film filled the fifteen-inch screen. For a moment, I pondered watching the porn parody in totality for a performance review. The moment passed as I jumped in the pool and began to stroke. In no time, the tingles bounced around my sensory system.

Like most of my sex life, I could see the end right from the beginning. My thighs tensed up as the swell made its way through my body. My lower body started to tremor, holding out as long as I could. Unfortunately, it was too late. The threshold had been crossed into the land of no return. My balls hit send and the gates flew open. With tissues wrapped tight around my raging salmon like a glove, I forged forward. My eyes squeezed close and time slowed down.

One.

Two.

Uh oh.

My penis *erupted*. Pump after pump of payload burst out of me in what can only be described as a yogurt tanker explosion.

Months of harvesting made their claim as the brevity of the male orgasm completed its cycle. This must be what a woman refers to when she has a full body orgasm. I've never witnessed one first hand, but I've heard this myth of a female orgasm more than once.

The last time I had a full body feeling like this was the second time I ever did Methylenedioxymethamphetamine, a drug known in the streets as MDMA. In clubs and festivals all over the world, it's known by its fitting white girl name, Molly or Mandy. I was with a group of friends at a music festival in upstate New York. We all washed down the bitter salty crystals and proceeded to dance in the rain to Big Gigantic, an electric funk band, and Kendrick Lamar, a poetic rapper. Drugs were used in a lot of scenarios, but they were made to be enjoyed while dancing in the rain with all your friends listening to rap music. It was every white girl's dream. Molly turned my pupils into portals and my feet into moonshoes. While most people went through this phase in high school or college, I waited years into my adult life to be a child. If people drank and did drugs early on, they usually settled down early on. If people like myself didn't drink or do drugs early on, that left the door wide open for fun later on. Both have their pros and their cons, but I was too old and poor to get addicted to anything at this point. Molly and I got along well because I love to dance, and it's physically impossible not to when there was music. Side effects included chewing a lot and jaw tension. Nothing good came free.

The first time I ever got high was my sophomore year of college. My friend Omar and I were rock radio DJs together and had finished a remote broadcast for a Paramore concert in Gainesville, Florida. As we sat in his apartment, his roommate passed around a pipe. Now, this was not the first time I had smoked weed. This was, however, the first time I got high. As previously stated, my body had a resilience to drugs, and weed was no different. There was a chance I might not have been smoking correctly, but that's another issue. Regardless, that shield of confidence pushed me to smoke a little more. I stood up to get some water when it hit. And I mean really hit. We moved to his room where I rotated sitting up and lying down in his bed. When I'm drunk, I have a protocol to sober up. Being high, I was lost. I couldn't have looked dumber from the outside. Stand up, walk in a circle, sit down. Omar, also high as a kite, went through the same rotation on an orange bean bag chair. No one who was really high ever wanted to admit how high they were until it was absolutely necessary. We sat in silence for two hours that night, just sitting up and lying down.

———

I lay there, exhausted, having completed my first squeeze in months. With a hand full of protein tissues, I knew I had to take a look. Did anything irregular come out of me? Were there cobwebs? Crustaceans? I tilt my head and look. To my delight, a healthy white consistency was slowly drying. No blood. Minimal amount of post-masturbation guilt. The gods of intercourse had reissued my passport. With a smile on my face and the tissues still in my hand, I rolled over and fell asleep elated. This must have been how it felt the first time some fifteen years ago.

26

BUT MY BODY'S TELLING ME YES

I could hear the Rocky theme music playing in the background. The first time overflowed with power, and the days' ensuing strokes weren't far off either. The time had come to battle a new boss and face my long time fear, a real live woman. The three-month mark passed and with it came the green light to have sex again. Who would help shepherd me back into intimacy? I wanted someone I could trust, but also who wouldn't judge me. I couldn't think of an active lover that would understand. After three months without contact, who would answer a booty call? Knowing the room for error, did I want to willingly subject a girl to the situation? I racked my brain for the least asshole-ish scenario and outcome.

The answer came to me a week before my birthday. History repeated itself and the universe provided me a familiar text message from none other than a bona fide sex ghost. This particular ghost I met on Halloween three years prior on Capitol Hill in Seattle. She took the most common female costume, a cat, and made it a little sexier by being a fox. Needless to say, she had a bushier tale. Lexi was cute, skinny, and, quite fittingly, sly. After a couple casual hang outs or dates, which were hard to tell the difference between sometimes, we hooked up.

Lexi was really cool except for one key issue. She was *terrible* in bed. When a guy is bad in bed, he fits the stereotype and gets to be the running joke for brunch all summer long. When a girl is bad in bed, it isn't funny. Guys have a filter. We would lie about it being good for both parties involved even if it wasn't. In all honesty, we probably already forgot we even had sex by the time it came up in conversation. Guys are dumb. We eat ribs, watch football, and get hypnotized by partial boobs. Lexi, though, she violated one of my key pillars for good sex. She had no rhythm. Either that or she was playing off of Dream Theater's 11/8 time signature.

Lexi also didn't make any sound during intercourse, which I also found problematic. Men sound dumb when they moan and grunt. Women sound sexy even though, especially in my case, they are usually faking it. Sounds were an indicator that at least one of the two or more parties involved were alive. Tight body, beautiful face, no sound. Once a woman moaned, it gave the man permission to let out dumb noises in echo. Lexi made zero sound. Casual sex had its pros and its cons, but these simple characteristics needed to be on the table before any serious commitments.

Lexi gifted me some of the most boring sex in my life, and that's why she was the perfect girl to re-lose my virginity to. I needed someone safe. No big movements, low expectations, perfectly vanilla. The universe provided.

Lexi
9:42pm: Hey! I'm coming to New York in two weeks. Are you going to be around? Would be fun to see you.

There's nothing wrong with vanilla. I love vanilla! Both genders have vanilla pitfalls we were susceptible to. If a guy wears a polo shirt tucked into his khakis, that's a vanilla move. If a girl curls her long hair with one of those dildo irons, that's a vanilla move. Of course, it can look good, but it's safe. There's nothing wrong with safe, and there's nothing wrong with vanilla. To Lexi's credit, she did have this trait that I couldn't imagine being common. Sometimes when she orgasmed, she'd go into an uncontrollable fit of laughter. Now I've had a lot of women laugh before, during, and after sex, but this was different. Heck, I've seen women try things that make me laugh myself soft. Sometimes I come so much, everyone laughs. But Lexi would cover her mouth and giggle like she was at a Def Comedy Jam. I guess Lexi's more vanilla bean. Maybe even French vanilla bean.

We bantered our way back into familiarity as I explained that my birthday was coming up. With an invite extended to crash, I prepared.

Preparation for meeting someone meant looking up and down their social profiles, playfully referred to as stalking. Lexi knew her angles better than most girls. I found her attractive in real life, but she was an absolute ten out of ten in photos. This presented a common modern day dilemma. Seeing used to be believing but now seeing could be misleading. Being photogenic wasn't a requirement to exist in the modern dating era but knowing your angles has become crucial. Lexi clearly photoshopped a couple of her pictures. No one's eye whites were *that* white, right? It's become so difficult to differentiate what's real and what's edited. Also, she had all these pictures by herself where she was looking off in the distance or she was laughing. Who was she laughing at? Why was she always kind of half looking down? Also, why was someone taking all these photos of you? I had to move to the tagged photos of her to get a better sense of reality, at which point I've spent an embarrassing amount of time looking at someone who I barely talked to. Even weirder, I had these imaginary conversations with Lexi in my head that I'd never say to her in person. Lexi happens to have a picture with this woman Sarah, who's this ultra blonde babe with millions of followers, and I go down the rabbit hole of her account. She loved to travel. I loved to travel! All of a sudden I'm having conversation with her in my head thinking about what a good match we'd make. What? This was why I stopped following Instagram models. My research (and tangents) didn't change the fact that she was coming, and I was ready for whatever version of her was going show up. At least, that's what I thought.

A wrench landed right in the middle of my game plan as she arrived to my apartment. She looked as attractive as she was when she was a fox in a bar, but something was different. Her bag hit the floor and we went in for the squeeze. With one prolonged embrace, my worst fears were confirmed. The two firm objects that pressed from her chest into mine were, in fact, two newly acquired boobs. The phrase "fake boobs" never sounded right to me. My theory was simple: if I could touch 'em, they were real. And their presence was very real. I'm not a boob man. I'm also not an ass man. I'm a man of balance. When given the choice for life, I'd take a butt for the simple reason that butts couldn't be bought easily. Fake boobs were an obvious red flag, mostly in younger women. My general rule of thumb for any augmentation was simple. It's okay as long as you were doing it for yourself, and not because of other external pressures like a boyfriend. If guys could augment their zip-zop, I have no doubt in my mind we would. That's for getting it bigger or smaller. Boobs of all sorts have their pros, cons, and superpowers, and all are fine by me. With Lexi's fresh set of mangos threatening her sweater, I couldn't tell if I was excited or if they'd become a problem. That being said, when a fake pair pressed into me, I get that magic tingle from my brain to my toes.

It. Is. On.

"Ooh easy there," she said as I hugged her tight, "I'm still getting used to these." As a common male tactic, I played dumb and pretended not to have gone through forty-five pages of internal dialogue in the past three seconds.

"Wait what?" I responded, with all the training a dropout actor could possibly have. I actively avoid calling them fake boobs because I still had PTSD from calling that stripper from Portland a stripper. You just never know, and I wasn't going to insult my way out of getting laid. New bongos for a girl who had zero tom toms her whole life had to be weird. Women who get them do love to show them off, which I, on behalf of straight men everywhere, appreciate. Even though the December chill kept her tots hidden, the chef downstairs started to heat up the stove.

"Are you crashing with me tonight?" I asked. Some people aren't huge on letting a partner sleep over, but I'm not one of them. Selfishly, I liked morning sex and was always looking to make use of the anatomic phenomenon known as morning wood. Thus, I would forgo the comfort of my own home for the possible comfort of a vagina. The low success rate of morning sex, which I understood, didn't deter me from hope. Women were self conscious and wanted to freshen up. I always woke up first and, thus, had time to brush my teeth, check my email, then hop back into bed and pretend like I was there the whole time. She'd ask how long I'd been up, and I'd lie to make her feel better about sleeping in. Was it creepy to hop back in bed and pretend I'd been asleep so when she woke up she felt more like it'd been a shared experience, thus increasing the chances of ringing in the morning with some vitamin D? Maybe, but I couldn't just lay there awake. I had shit to do!

———

We met up with some friends for dinner at a Filipino spot in the East Village. Sitting around the table were the cast and crew that had been there all along my arduous journey. We feasted on an array of meats and rice in honor of my impending return. My birthday had turned into a celebration of another kind this time around. I worried that the delicious food would cause cramping during re-entry, but my reasoning wasn't fully back in check. Lexi, sitting to my left, gave my leg a double squeeze. This was the equivalent to the old timey movies where a guy raised his eyebrows twice really fast at a cute girl. I squeezed back, and the rest of dinner fast forwarded. Fifteen minutes later, we were climbing the fateful stairwell, which doubled as a mountain right after surgery. I unlocked my front door as she pressed her newly acquired missiles into my back.

The blood flowed south from my brain. As my ballast filled, discomfort panged the inside of my shaft. The pain reminded me where this started and suddenly I'm fighting off PenisTSD. The first task was to keep my mind from usurping blood back up to the brain. Mental Erectile Dysfunction, or MED, was when my mind was telling me no, but my body... *my body* was telling me yes. As Lexi kissed my neck, the fire alarm sounded. It. Was. On.

I sent my hands in formation across her body. *ATTACK!* I commanded. She sent her hands back at my body on a strong counter attack. With a Kung Fu grip, she grabbed a hold of my joystick and started playing games. Her dry hand on my dry "leg" didn't feel bad, but it sure didn't feel good. I would've suggested licking her hand, but I've always been too polite for in-flight feedback. I thought *lick your hand* really hard. Nothing. Time to flip it before I lost my erection. Time was money shots, people. We had to move. I used directional kissing, a technique I learned in the Congo, to get her onto my ever-taunting bed. For months, this bed had laughed at me as I laid helplessly on it, poking around a hard dick like a piñata void of candy. Finally, the time had come to get that candy. She started to unbutton her top. That fateful moment of what her new boobs looked like was upon me. My pointer and middle finger play DJ on her scratch box in hopes to expedite the process. For a brief moment, I looked for the G spot. *Where the hell is this thing?* Her top was already off, yet the bra persisted.

I sent my hands in equal but opposite formation around her body. *THE BRA!* I commanded. Held together by a mysterious clasp, her demoralizing bra strap laughed at me. A guy has five seconds to get a woman's bra off before she does it herself. Removing a woman's bra has always been a catch-22. If the guy removes a bra too easily, the woman will think he's done it too many times. If the guy can't remove a bra, she'll wonder how he was going to satisfy the rest of her desires. Actually, she'd probably just take it off and keep going. As a gametime decision, I unsnap her bra because life was short and boobs were awesome. We both paused and took in the newfound melons on her chest.

"What do you think?" She asked. I cupped each tot from the side and tilted my head in examination. There was only one answer to this question.

"I think they're grrreeat!" I said with absolution. After all those years of eating Frosted Flakes, my Tony-the-Tiger impression finally paid off. Even if I thought they weren't symmetrical, I wasn't about to let honesty ruin my birthday. My clothes came off alarmingly fast, including my socks. I took my socks off first, actually. I never trusted someone who left their socks on during sex. The only exceptions were those knee-high socks girls wore, and even that was weird if she did it more than once. With us both naked, the right of passage was ready to take place.

This was it. It was time to dock the ship. Rock the casbah. Bump uglies. Do the hokey-pokey. Make bacon. Bump and grind. Boom boom in her zoom zoom. Stuff the turkey. Feed the cat. And most importantly, sail the seven seas without cracking a plank. I could hear the aptly named Neil Armstrong calling in my head. *One small step for man.* The boosters fired off to center the shuttle. NASA's headquarters called into my brain. *Be very gentle.* The doctor's warning played back over and over in my mind. I had to play this right if I ever wanted to be in this stratosphere again. As the tip touched her empanada, the weatherman signaled that the conditions were right.

With a nod to Sheryl Sandberg, I leaned in and watched months of hard work manifest. I breached the door and, just like that, I was in! We did it, and we were doing it. The hard part was over, but the notion that either of us would finish was up in the air. Occasionally, she moaned. Had she gone to dirty talk, I probably would not have reciprocated. I'm sure guys say weird things in bed, but I've never been a big talker. Lexi was a beautiful human to look at, and maybe that's why she kept it simple. She briefly got on top, but remained unapologetically calm. For a hot second, she started grinding hard. With a thunderous grip, I put my hand upon her hips. We did not dip. Instead, I kept her from imitating one of those rap guys' girlfriends. She made a couple more noises and right as I felt her body tense up, she collapsed over to my side. She started her familiar giggle, and I took creative liberty to assume that was because she had orgasmed. She looked over at me, waiting for me to roll over and remount, or rearrange into a pretzel, or put her on all fours. I did no such thing.

"Did you finish?" She asked, a bit out of breath.

"No, I'm good," I said as I pulled her in and laughed a bit, "I don't have to always finish."

Truth be told, I had finished, but not in the way she expected. The smile on my face proved the sincerity of my satisfaction. Looking down at Lucky, I knew he was proud too. Sure, the pain of stretching skin and fresh sutures persisted with each heartbeat, but it didn't matter. I had sex. I felt the tingles. I kept it all in one piece. Of all the gin joints, this one didn't need an ambulance.

27

THE END IS THE BEGINNING

How many people get two penises in one lifetime? That's what went through my brain six months later as I scrolled through the medical bills. After all the surgeries and treatments, my new dick ended up costing $60,000. My dick was worth $60,000. I don't know if that was a lot, but it sure was cool to attach a tangible number to it. Because of insurance, my out of pocket costs were much lower, but I think this would've qualified under the catastrophic policy had this happened ten years earlier.

I was eternally grateful to whatever higher power had granted me mercy. Something, somewhere gave me the miracle of a renewed sex life. Whether it was the credit I had built up from Jesus camp or not, I'd never been more thankful. Sex, of course, changed forever. I would no longer heed the call of a woman who wanted it harder or faster, instead I would stick to the advice of the various medical staff I'd encountered. Sex, or lack thereof, represented something different to everyone. I started late and made up for lost time. I've used it as a means for pleasure and pain, love and hate, humor and tragedy. My friends and family showed up in a way I could only dream of. Even Parker, whom I had really hurt, wanted the best for me. My life had a new lens on it, and these are my lessons learned (part two).

Lesson One: Be nice. You never know what someone is going through or has been through. Don't be quick to judge somebody just because they're rude or not particularly pleasant. I'll mutter under my breath about slow walkers, but they won't end the world. A random smile or a small act of kindness can go a long way. If someone would hold the door, or pick up something I dropped, it gave me that much more faith in humanity. We've all got something, and the weight they carry shouldn't be compared to our own reality.

Lesson Two: Be thankful. The fact that we're alive is a miracle. I have fully functional limbs. I can walk, talk, hear, and see. Every single time I pee, I thank God in all his or her forms that I was able to come back from the dead. I am thankful that I can shower unassisted. The little things had been big things. The phrase 'give thanks' came with a bit of an eye roll when we think about how taxing it would be to appreciate all the gifts we're born with. All I know is that the world slowed down when I had a catheter in my pee hole. When the world slowed down, it was easy to appreciate its intricacies and its simplicities.

Lesson Three: Doctors are miracle workers. We are mere flesh and bones. We bend and break. Things can go horribly wrong in an instant. When those things happen, doctors somehow manage to put us back together on a daily basis. Although I barely knew them, two men decided to go through years of medical school, residency, and practice so that they were equipped to put me back together properly. I'm not really sure how to thank doctors in general, but I hope all my insurance money is a good place to start.

Lesson Four: Be careful when fxcking. This should be obvious by now. I don't care how long you've spent in the gym or how many protein shakes you've had, the bedroom is not a place to flex. Muscles tear no matter how strong any of us are and that's a fact. They're clinging on to our bones by threads. Even the slightest push in the wrong direction can make them snap. Separate porn and real life. Separate the gym and the bedroom. Seriously, proceed with caution. You have been warned.

Lesson Five: It can always be worse. It really, truly always can. I didn't beat cancer. I'm not living in a warzone. People are fighting for their life every day, some worse than others but each in their own right. Somehow, I won the lottery. Somehow, a lot of us won the lottery. It didn't take snapping my peapod to make me realize that, but we often need reminders of what we already know. I was alive. Anyone who has been through some sort of surgery or accident knows that life is not a given. Murphy's Law ripped through my life more times than I can count, but, at the end of the day, it could always be worse.

After six months as a handicapped senior citizen, those were my closing reflections. My body had done all the recovering it was going to do. My scar still makes me laugh every time I look at it, which is a lot. This story still makes me laugh. The truth is usually funnier and by telling my friends... by telling *you*, I will have hopefully prevented this tragedy from happening. So far that's been true, and I hope that never changes. I hope there is no sequel to this. I hope that no one can ever relate to what I've been through. I hope that no girl has to be on the other end of this as the lover or the one being loved. If I have my way, this will be the last broken banana the world ever sees again.

———

LAST PAGE FIRST

For all the assholes out there that read the last page first (me), here's the scoop. I tore two muscles in my wedding tackle and *severed* my urethra having sex. There was blood, pain, love, frustration, solidarity, support, and hilarity everywhere. Tied to a catheter, the world around me slowed down in a way that adjusted my perspective on life. I've always believed the two elements that bring people perspective are travel and fragility, of which this is most certainly the latter.

Both physically and emotionally, people are fragile. Life is tough! We spend so much time trying to live a normal life, and this story is about how fucking weird life really is. How weird *we* are. And let me tell you, we are *all* weird. I've tried so hard to be normal because sometimes it's easier. It's easier to talk about the weather. It's easier to believe what I've always believed. It's easier to act like women don't poop and old people don't have sex. Unfortunately, life ain't easy and everyone's got a wicked scar to prove it. Mine happens to look like a cheap plastic tie stapled around an unbaked baguette, but it's no different than anyone else's. Scars are tattoos that we didn't ask for, and my scar is about a simple truth. We aren't as normal as we look.

The last page should tell you how the story ends, but I don't know how it ends. I do know that 98.5% of this is 100% accurate, and people will judge my relationships and choices based on their own reality. You might read this and think "he deserved it," to which I would be like "that's cool." Sometimes, I think that too.

Parker and I hadn't found any solutions to our feelings, and no closure to our situation. The end of that story, if it ends at all, hasn't been written. I do know that everything we do revolves around the ones we love, and this was no different.

I don't know what will happen with my love life or my sex life, but they will certainly have their ups and downs.* The world will end sooner or later, so we might as well laugh a little while we cry. We might as well play with ourselves when no one's around. We might as well take a look in our brains and realize the truth can be refreshing if we're brave enough to claim it. If this is truly where you're starting then I hope you've enjoyed it because, like my sex life, I'm already finished.